NEW MONASTICISM

WHAT IT HAS TO SAY TO TODAY'S CHURCH

JONATHAN WILSON-HARTGROVE

BrazosPress

a division of Baker Publishing Group
Grand Rapids, Michigan

© 2008 by Jonathan Wilson-Hartgrove

Published by Brazos Press
a division of Baker Publishing Group
P.O. Box 6287, Grand Rapids, MI 49516-6287
www.brazospress.com

Printed in the United States of America

Library of Congress Cataloging-in-Publication Data
Wilson-Hartgrove, Jonathan, 1980–
    New monasticism : what it has to say to today's church / Jonathan Wilson-Hartgrove.
      p. cm.
    ISBN 978-1-58473-224-8 (pbk.)
    1. Christian life. 2. Church. 3. Monastic and religious life. I. Title.
BV4501.3.W5565 2008
255—dc22   2007042625

For Marti and Jonathan,
who've watched and prayed

I am not in a position to state who is guilty and who is innocent. I am not a judge or a magistrate. Worse still, I am a priest; my duty towards believers is not to try them or to sentence them, but to help them find their way.

—Andre Sibomana, Rwandan priest
who survived the 1994 genocide

CONTENTS

READING THE SIGNS OF THE TIMES

I'm part of a movement called new monasticism. I don't wear a robe and I'm happily married, which is enough to confuse most people. If you'll bear with me for a few pages, I'll try to make clear what I mean by "new monasticism." For now, just know that it brings me into contact with all kinds of American Christians. And almost everywhere I go these days, people agree that something is wrong in American Christianity. Whether I'm talking to Pentecostals or Presbyterians, Democrats or Republicans, academics in a coffee shop or neighbors on their front porch, there seems to be a consensus on this: the church in America isn't living up to what it's supposed to be. Somehow we've lost our way.

Now, the minute I try to get specific about what the problem is or solicit ideas about how to fix it, this fragile consensus crumbles into the rhetorical rubble of the culture wars or the impasse of partisan politics. One side says our moral fabric has worn thin and we have to defend the family. The other says we're drunk on war and we need to defend the poor. Both camps circle their wagons and insist that their concerns are most important. And pretty soon the conversation is over. Or it turns into a yelling match. Either way, there isn't much hope that the world will know we are Christians by our love for one another. Often we can't even agree that we're all Christian.

Which makes it pretty hard to take Jesus at his word. Because whatever else Jesus may have been about here on earth, it seems pretty clear from all accounts that he came to make it possible for those who believe in him to be reconciled to one another and to God. Here's how Paul says it in his letter to the Ephesians: "Now in Christ Jesus you who once were far off have been brought near by the blood of Christ. . . . He has abolished the law with its commandments and ordinances, that he might create in himself one new humanity in place of the two, thus making peace, and might reconcile both groups to God" (2:13–16). Paul isn't appealing to Jews and Gentiles, begging them to be united because they serve the same God. He's saying that they've already been made one. That's what happened in Jesus. Fragmented peoples can have a relationship with God because they have already been reconciled in a new humanity.

When the Holy Spirit came on the early church at Antioch, Jews and Gentiles alike trusted Jesus to give them access to God. United in worship, they shared life with one another like a family. No one quite knew what to make of this at first. They knew what a group of Jews was supposed to be, and they knew what Gentiles looked like, but they weren't sure what to call Jews and Gentiles living and worshiping together in Jesus's name. So they decided to make up a new name. They called them "Christians," Acts says (11:26).

Unity across dividing lines was what distinguished the early church—so much so that they required a new name. Christianity was a new identity, neither Jew nor Gentile, male nor female, slave nor free (Gal. 3:28). That's pretty incredible to think about, especially in a church fractured by schisms and creeds, denominational divides and ethnic identities. It's hard for anybody in America to look at the first Christians and feel very proud about where we are now.

Tragic as our situation may be, though, I think we may have reached a point of clarity here at the dawn of a new millennium. At the risk of focusing too much on the negative, I want to begin with something that almost everyone in the church acknowledges: it's hard to be a Christian in America.

Maybe it's a little disturbing to think that our difficulty at being Christian is what most unites the church. When it comes to least common denominators, that seems pretty low. But it's worth noting that we haven't always had this in common. As a matter of fact, much of evangelism in the twentieth century was an attempt to convince Americans of just the opposite—that it's *easy* to be Christian in this land of promise. At the opening of the twentieth century, crusaders of the so-called Christian Century heralded the progress of science and civilization, anticipating that they were closer than they had ever been to ushering in the kingdom of God. A few decades later, evangelicals started to employ the new technologies of television and radio to invite people to make a simple choice for Jesus from the comfort of their home. All their listeners needed to do was believe. Christianity couldn't be easier than it was here in the land of the free and home of the brave.

But somewhere along the way, despite the promise of scientific progress and the freedom of democratic society, the signs of the times began to change. The "war to end all wars" was followed by a second world war that destroyed Europe, introduced the Bomb, and, most tragically perhaps, saw Christians kill fellow Christians by the millions. Still, we called that the "good war." Vietnam was the quagmire that broke America's spirit of optimism, sending baby boomers reeling with a series of revolutions, searching for some place to put their feet on the ground. Evangelical Christianity, which had gone underground fifty years earlier after the embarrassment of the Scopes Monkey Trial, reemerged as a political force bent on restoring the Judeo-Christian values that had been flouted by progressives. But conservative Christians proved no better than the liberals at stewarding political power or finding an identity that was distinctly Christian. At the beginning of the twenty-first century, Americans are free to be Christian Republicans or Christian Democrats (and they choose to be each in increasingly equal numbers). But we can see more clearly than ever before, perhaps, just how hard it is for any of us to pledge our ultimate allegiance to Jesus. *Christian* has become an adjective that we tack onto some more fundamental identity. We don't use the word like they did at Antioch, to describe a peculiar people. We don't use it that way because we can feel how hard it really is to be a Christian in America.

Stumbling to Follow Jesus

Much of my generation grew up with this sense that we were living in a post-Christian era. But I'll have to confess that I didn't. I was raised the son of Southern Baptists in King, North Carolina, one of those last bastions of Christendom between the ever-expanding holes in America's Bible Belt. Born in 1980, I was born again while Reagan was still in the White House. Where I grew up we talked about Jesus like he lived just over the next hill, across from the Flints' place. My people taught me to love God and memorize scripture, and I did as I was told. By the time I was in high school, I was certain the Lord had called me to lead the nation in Jesus's name by becoming president of the United States. While still a student in high school, I made my way to DC to work as a page for Strom Thurmond, then president pro tempore of the U.S. Senate.

But in my rush to follow Jesus to the White House, I almost tripped over him one day on my way to lunch at Union Station. Just outside the doors of that great building, a man was crouched down, holding a Styrofoam cup. He asked if I could spare some change, and I looked at him without saying a word. I remembered what I'd heard back in King about how poor folks in the city were lazy and begged money to buy drugs and booze. A country boy in the city, I was dressed in my Sunday best, doing everything I knew how to fit in. I didn't want to look naive. So I looked straight through the man and kept walking.

But about the time I stepped through those glass doors into Union Station, I recalled one of my memory verses from vacation Bible school. They were the words of Jesus, ringing in my head: "Verily I say unto you, inasmuch as ye did it not to one of the least of these, ye did it not to me" (Matt. 25:45 KJV). I knew that if those words were true, I had not only just ignored a fellow human being; I had completely missed the Lord I was trying to serve. I turned around and ran all the way back to my little dorm room on Capitol Hill, found one of the Billy Graham tracts my church had sent with me to the big city, wrapped a twenty-dollar bill around it, and returned to Union Station to deposit it in that man's Styrofoam cup. It was the only thing I could think to do at the time. I just didn't want to miss Jesus.

That experience got me thinking about the tension between the ways I had imagined following Jesus and the things Jesus taught about how to live with God in the world. I thought Jesus wanted me to get up at 4 a.m. and work as hard as I could every day to prove that I was good enough to run the United States of America. But in my rush to achieve power and fight for justice and truth, I had rushed right past Jesus as he begged with a Styrofoam cup. Jesus said, "Blessed are the poor, for theirs is the kingdom of God," but I was rooming with a Congressman's son, trying to hide my hick accent and prove that I could hang with rich boys "in the loop." Jesus said, "Blessed are the peacemakers," but I was carrying session notes to the Senate Armed Service Committee and listening to discussions about appropriations for the world's largest military. Jesus said, "Blessed are the pure in heart," but I was lusting after everything I laid my eyes on and starting to feel as if that was what this whole page program was about.

I remember Lloyd John Ogilvie, chaplain of the Senate at the time, saying that before leaving to return home one of the pages had told him that he would be back, only next time he would have a seat on the Senate floor. "Just don't let it cost you

your soul," Ogilvie had replied. When I heard that, I started to
realize just how hard it is to be a Christian in America.

Signs That It's Hard to Be a Christian

Jesus said that when the sky is red in the morning, sailors
take warning, but when it's red at night, sailors delight (Matt.
16:2–3, Southern folk wisdom paraphrase). His point, I take it,
was that people who make their living on the seas know how
to read the natural signs. They pay attention to what's going
on around them, and they can anticipate what's coming before
it happens. Bob Dylan captured the notion succinctly when
he suggested that most people don't need a meteorologist "to
know which way the wind blows."

But Jesus accused his listeners of not having such good common sense, because they were always asking him for a sign. He
said they were a "wicked and adulterous generation," begging
for some miraculous sign while ignoring the plain and simple
signs that anyone could see. Those signs, Jesus said, made it
plain enough that a storm was brewing on the political scene,
that there was corruption in the economic sphere, that the
temple was filled with hypocrites, and that God's people had
strayed far from their calling. Life can't go on like this very long,
Jesus said. The end is near. Whoever can read the signs of the
time ought to turn from the wrath that is to come.

But even if we have a sense that there's something wrong
with the way things are going in the world, most of us worry
about people who talk like Jesus did. On this side of Y2K, we
know not to trust people who say the world is about to end.
Maybe we wish things were different. Maybe we even think
it's our responsibility to change some things. But "Repent:
the end is near" sounds a little extreme. Two thousand years
after Jesus's ascension into heaven, it looks like he was more
right than even he knew when he said, "About that day or
hour no one knows" when the end will come (Mark 13:32).
We like to think that Jesus was just a little overzealous with

his warnings about the end. Maybe he exaggerated to make a point.

But if we listen to what Jesus said about the signs of the times, his language isn't overblown. He doesn't claim to have special knowledge. He doesn't rely on classified reports or sophisticated data analysis. Jesus appeals to common sense. He quotes folk wisdom. If you'll just look at what's happening in the world, Jesus says, you'll see that something's wrong. The world isn't working the way God made it to work. Something has to change. Either that, or the end is near.

Here at the dawn of the third millennium, I'm convinced that we face a crisis very similar to the one Jesus saw and named in first-century Palestine. The end of the world is near. Unless we repent and find a new way of life, we are bound to destroy ourselves. Some political scientists and environmentalists have intricate and well-researched arguments to make this same basic point. Many fundamentalist Christians have lists of proof-texts that they like to quote to say essentially the same thing. But I think Jesus was right: all we really need to do is read the signs of the times. Here's a brief look at five that we've all seen or heard about.

Wars and rumors of wars. The United States declared war on terror in 2001 and said that our national security demanded aerial bombardment, invasion, and occupation of Iraq in 2003. Leaders of almost every major denomination of the church said that such an invasion would be unjust. Nevertheless, hundreds of thousands of Christians were deployed to the Middle East to fight. The church could not imagine any alternative. It is worth remembering that both Democrats and Republicans supported America's "war on terror" and voted to grant George Bush power to go to war in Iraq. I don't want to argue politics. I just want to read our war-making as a sign of the times for the church in America. We were and continue to be powerless to do what our just war tradition and practically all of our bishops say we should do. It is a sign to us of just how hard it is to be Christian in America.

The color line. Where I live in the South, signs used to mark some water fountains "white" and others "colored." People with

black skin could not drink from a "white" water fountain. Those
signs are gone, but a color line still marks the landscape in
America. Everyone knows that to cross certain streets is to go
from a black neighborhood to a white neighborhood. Schools
in the South were integrated more than thirty years ago, but
many of our neighborhoods never were. Neither were most
of our churches.

After Hurricane Katrina hit New Orleans in 2005, I heard
about a white minister in North Carolina who, when he saw
the initial news coverage of the refugees in the Superdome,
commented to his wife that he didn't know New Orleans was
such a black city. Of course it wasn't. Poor African Americans
were left behind by fellow citizens of New Orleans who only
thought to look out for themselves. Horrible as it is, though,
human selfishness should not surprise us. We know that people
are broken by sin. What we cannot forget about Katrina is that
almost no white Christians stopped on their way out of New
Orleans to offer a ride to their black sisters and brothers. The
real tragedy is that it didn't even occur to them—and that it
most likely would not occur to the rest of us if Katrina happened
in our town. The pervading color line that divides the church
is a sign to us that when the pressure is on, the blood of our
racial identity runs thicker than the water of our baptism.

Immigration. I've been to southern Arizona and stood beside
the wall that our government built on the southern border of
the United States to keep people from immigrating illegally.
Within the logic of nation-state politics and democratic capitalism, it makes sense that a country must defend its borders,
control immigration, and protect its economic interests. Debates between liberals and conservatives in American politics
have been about how best to do this. But as people adopted into
the family of God, U.S. Christians share our most fundamental
citizenship with brothers and sisters from Mexico and Latin
America who are being forced by economic pressures to leave
family and home, risk death in the desert, and work illegally
in the United States. Catholics are faced with this sign even
more clearly than most Americans. Go to Mass in any U.S.

city—or many rural parishes in farm areas, for that matter—
and look who is eating at the Lord's table. Jesus says, "I was
hungry and you gave me food, . . . I was a stranger and you
welcomed me" (Matt. 25:35). But America calls that "harbor-
ing an illegal alien." The signs of the times say it's hard to be
Christian in America.

Abortion. Catholics and evangelicals are right to insist that
the millions of children who have been aborted in America
are a sign to us that something is deeply broken about our
way of life. The fact of the matter is, though, that it is not for
the most part pro-choice feminists who are opting to end
pregnancies for convenience's sake (it is, after all, easier to
just use birth control if you choose to be sexually active). The
vast majority of women who have abortions don't feel they
have much of a choice in a society where it is extremely difficult to raise children without two incomes, and even more
difficult if the father has chosen to move on. And many of
these women are Christian. The church of Jesus Christ, which
was noted in the ancient world for taking in children who had
been abandoned to exposure, has not been able to take care
of its own poor and single mothers here in America. For the
woman who grieves her abortion and for the nuclear family
with 2.2 kids that has no room for their poor sister, it's hard
to be a Christian in America.

Billboards. When reading the signs of the times, we ought
not overlook the literal signs that beg for our attention everywhere we look. They are so common that we easily become de-
sensitized to them. The brilliant creations of marketers, ads tap
into our deepest desires and seek to convince us that what we
really want is whatever they are selling. If you want to know the
power of billboards, take a picture of the most outlandish one
you see this week. Think for a minute about how that picture
is inviting you to imagine yourself (if you're a man, you might
think about how it invites your sister to reimagine herself).
Then put the picture away for a year. The incredible thing is that
when you look at it again, it won't look nearly as unbelievable.
Often it will look strikingly like people you know.

When I was a teenager (less than a decade ago), the girls in our youth group had to wear one-piece bathing suits to summer camp, the assumption being, I guess, that the bare stomachs of Christian young women would lead to unholy thoughts in the minds of Christian young men (which was probably true, since there were more than enough unholy thoughts among us without exposed midriffs). None of this seemed strange to me ten years ago. But I was reminded how quickly things change when I was invited to talk to a youth group recently and, lo and behold, right there in the church fellowship hall every other fourteen-year-old was flashing a bare midriff. I doubt the minds of young Christian men have gotten much holier in the past decade. But I have enough fatherly impulses in my late twenties that I wanted to cry. In a culture obsessed with sex and self-fulfillment, our church hasn't found a way to help its young men and women want something different from the self-image Madison Avenue sells them.

Praying in the Belly of a Paradox

So both the conservative and the liberal critics are right: there's something wrong with the church in America. We're failing on family values, and we're failing to care for our poor brothers and sisters. We struggle to find the inner peace that comes from a personal relationship with Jesus, and we're unable to make the peace that allows for human flourishing in society. In our own camps, when our guard is down, we all seem to be confessing the same thing: it's hard to be a Christian in America.

But what kind of news is that? It hardly sounds like good news to hear that the dividing wall between left and right in the church has broken down because the whole building has collapsed. Sure, we're starting to break out of some of our old patterns. But our eyes are opening to find that the church is in ruins around us. We cling to fragments of a tradition we know to be true, trying desperately to somehow put the pieces

together again. Catholics try charismatic renewal while evangelicals experiment with *lectio divina*. Meanwhile, everyone
worries about both the Crusades and the televangelists. Bits
of truth seem scattered abroad in almost every corner of the
church, but the glaring faults of each tradition make our faith
feel incoherent. So many Christians in America today feel para-
lyzed by the paradox of a church that promises so much yet
seems so hard to find in reality.

When the scribes and Pharisees in Jesus's day kept begging
him for a sign, he scolded them for not knowing how to read
the signs of the times. But he didn't refuse their request al-
together. He said they wouldn't be given any sign *except* the
sign of Jonah. Of course they all knew the story about how God
had called Jonah to cry out against Nineveh, and how Jonah had
decided instead to quietly slip on down to the shore and catch
the first boat headed in the opposite direction. As if trying to
get as far as possible from the God of heaven, Jonah went down
into the bowels of the ship and fell asleep. But when a storm
like they'd never seen before was about to destroy the crew
and all their cargo, they hauled Jonah up and asked him what
the gods had against him. Rather than repent of his rebellion
against Yahweh, Jonah told the men that he was running from
the God of heaven and opted to go down even farther—down
into the sea, where he was swallowed by a giant fish.

Right about then, things weren't looking so good for Jonah.
You might say he'd reached rock bottom. But it was just when
Jonah had run as far from God as he could that he decided to
pray to God. And God heard his prayers. The fish spat Jonah
out, and he rose up and went to Nineveh, according to the word
of the Lord. The word God gave Jonah to preach was brief, but
those scribes Jesus was talking to had devoted their lives to the
study of words, so they would have caught its clever double
meaning: "Forty days more, and Nineveh will be *over*turned"—   ✳
or turned *around* (Jonah 3:4 NIV). Nineveh was about to be
either destroyed or converted. It could mean either one. The
paradoxical prophet proclaimed a message of judgment and
hope at the same time. The end of the world as they knew it in

Nineveh was also the beginning of something new. In the ruins of an old life lay the promise of new life with God.

Jesus refused to offer any sign other than the sign of Jonah, but he proved that sign to be enough by performing it in his death and resurrection. Paul captures the paradox well: "For our sake he made him to be sin who knew no sin, so that in him we might become the righteousness of God" (2 Cor. 5:21). The author of life submitted himself to death, and just as Jonah was three days in the belly of the whale before he got up and went to Nineveh, so too did Jesus on the third day rise from the dead. He gave us the sign of resurrection.

Twentieth-century Trappist monk Thomas Merton wrote that the life of "every Christian is signed with the sign of Jonah, because we all live by the power of Christ's resurrection."[1] The sign that marks the life of the church in the world is God's victory over death through death—the ultimate winning by losing. Any church that remembers its identity in the transition from Good Friday to Easter morning has reason to hope, even in the darkest night. Yes, it's hard to be a Christian in America. Indeed, the church we know is fraught with contradictions. But God is able to restore life, giving warmth to limbs that were frozen in death. Even if the church is the dead and broken body of Christ, God can resurrect it.

It is hard for the church to remember God's resurrection power. In the New Testament, Paul writes to the Ephesians, praying that they will know "what is the immeasurable greatness of [God's] power for us who believe, according to the working of his great power. God put this power to work in Christ when he raised him from the dead" (Eph. 1:19–20). Evidently those early converts to Christianity at Ephesus had a hard time remembering God's power over death. So too with American Christianity today. But throughout the history of the church God has called people to pray as Paul did for grace to remember what Christ's resurrection means for the church. Merton, who was heir to a long monastic tradition of prophetic witness, articulated his

1. Thomas Merton, *The Sign of Jonas* (New York: Image, 1956), 7.

sense of vocation this way: "I feel that my own life is especially sealed with this great sign . . . because like Jonah himself I find myself traveling toward my destiny in the belly of a paradox."[2]

In the belly of the paradox that is American Christianity, I believe God is moving to create new monastic communities to help the church in America remember resurrection. This is a book about that movement of the Spirit and what it has to say to the wider church. Though the signs of the time suggest that it's hard to be a Christian in America, there are also signs that God is doing something new in places that have been overlooked and abandoned by our society. Stumbling to follow Jesus myself, I found my way into some of these communities and learned to read the Bible anew with them. The story of the people of God came alive in that context, and I began to see how God has moved through the centuries to remind the church of its true identity through monastic movements. Monasticism, I learned, isn't about achieving some sort of individual or communal piety. It's about helping the church be the church.

This is a book about a movement I have been caught up in, so I won't pretend to be unbiased. This story has changed my life. I share it with you, however, because it is not about me. It's not even just about the couple thousand people who are living in new monastic communities around the country. This is a book about what it means to be Christian as citizens of the world's last remaining superpower at the beginning of the third millennium.

Once we realize that it's hard to be Christian in America, it's easier to remember that none of us can do it on our own. We need each other, and we need God. We need the same power that raised Jesus from the dead. The good news is that even amidst the fragments of the church we're called to be, we have that power. In the first half of this book (chapters 2–4), I look at signs that point to God's stirring up a new monasticism in American Christianity. I go on to explore the roots

2. Ibid. Note: I have changed Merton's variant spelling "Jonas" to "Jonah" in this quotation.

of this movement in historic monastic movements as well as the story of the people of God in Scripture. In the way that I most like to argue (by telling a string of stories), I try to show that God has consistently helped the church remember who it is through monastic movements. In the second half of the book (chapters 5–9), I take a closer look at the practices of new monastic communities, asking what the wider church might glean from our little experiments in faithfulness. I don't pretend that new monastic communities hold the answer to every challenge that faces the church today. I only want to bear witness to God's resurrection power, which we have glimpsed and delighted in. We have seen that the sign of Jonah reappears wherever we're willing to embrace the paradox of the cross and trust God alone to save us. As Don Mosley of Jubilee Partners in Comer, Georgia, writes after twenty five years in neomonastic community, "That's not merely wishful thinking. That's reality. We know what we are talking about. We have seen it with our own eyes!"[3]

---

3. Don Mosley with Joyce Hollyday, *With Our Own Eyes* (Scottdale, PA: Herald, 1996), 293.

2

SEEING SIGNS OF SOMETHING NEW

We were halfway up a thirteen-mile trail in the Adirondack Mountains when Leah asked me if I had ever heard of "the Simple Way." I had just met Leah and her friend Sarah. It was the week before we were to start our first year at Eastern College, a Christian liberal arts school outside of Philadelphia. The school had sent us out into the wilderness to get to know each other, and a thirteen-mile hike offered plenty of time to talk. My aching legs made any simple way sound appealing. "Tell me about it," I said.

Leah and Sarah started talking about a group of recent Eastern graduates who shared a house in an abandoned neighborhood of Philadelphia. During their time as students, these five friends had read a newspaper article about some homeless families who were being evicted from an abandoned Catholic cathedral in the city. "They're trying to kick Jesus out of the church," one of them said, echoing the words of Jesus that had rung in my head outside Union Station: "Inasmuch as ye have done it unto one of the least of these my brethren, ye have done it unto me" (Matt. 25:40 KJV). After some conversation, the students had decided to ride down to the cathedral and see what was going on.

What they saw changed them. White college students who had grown up in the suburbs met people they had previously known only as "poor and homeless." Inside the abandoned church building, they recognized these strangers as brothers and sisters, fellow members of God's family. They shared the Lord's Supper together. They sang freedom songs. They became friends. And eventually the students moved into the neighborhood to become the Simple Way community. They didn't start any programs or solicit sponsorship from a mission agency. They simply said they wanted to "love God, love people, and follow Jesus."

Leah and Sarah had visited the house, had met the community, and were impressed by how they lived out their faith in unassuming but authentic ways. They wanted to introduce me to the Simple Way when we got back to Philadelphia. I said I thought it sounded interesting, and we continued our hike.

But I kept thinking about the story they had told me. Ever since I'd stumbled into Jesus outside Union Station, I'd been asking God to show me what it meant to follow Jesus. I could see that it was hard to be a Christian in America, but I also believed that it must be possible. Surely Jesus would not say "Follow me" without also making a way for us to do it. I was looking for a way to live that would make it easier for me to do the things that Jesus taught and practiced. The story about the Simple Way stuck in my mind like the nagging but innocent voice of a kid who won't stop asking her parents "Why?" I wanted to see what this way of life looked like.

On our first weekend at Eastern College, I rode into Philadelphia with Leah and Sarah to meet the Simple Way. Their house sat in the V-intersection of two streets with a storefront on the corner. A cardboard sign in the store window read "The Gathering" and quoted Acts 4 at the bottom: "They shared what they had in common and no one among them had need." Inside there was indeed a gathering of people and stuff, arranged (or not) in a rather disorderly fashion. A group of people were chatting beside a shelf of used books in one corner while a couple of folks slumped on a couch in another. A few women were digging through boxes of secondhand clothing. The mosaic on the wall said "The Simple Way," but it looked a lot more like a mess.

Over the next few years I became accustomed to that mess, came to love the people at the Simple Way, and learned to re-read the Bible in that place. Christ's command to "welcome the stranger" made sense here where the homeless were invited in for conversation over a cup of coffee. "Love one another" wasn't just about being nice but meant learning to negotiate the real differences between people who were trying to live together. "The one who had much did not have too much" came to life as people shared their incomes and their stuff (see 2 Cor. 8:15, Exod. 16:18). It seemed like the Bible was speaking directly to questions that came up in daily life at the Simple Way.

I remember reading a passage by the German theologian Dietrich Bonhoeffer. "The more genuine and deeper our community becomes," he wrote, "the more will everything else between us recede, the more clearly and purely will Jesus Christ and his work become the one and only thing that is vital between us."[1] Bonhoeffer's words rang true because I could see and feel the community he was talking about. One night as I prayed in my dorm room, the Holy Spirit stirred me deeply. "The light that broke forth was of a different sort," I wrote in my journal. "It was a light of hope that shone as if after the twilight. . . . My American Jesus joined Nietzsche's god in the graves of Europe tonight. Yes, that god is dead. Now, let us dance. What Bonhoeffer has invited me into is the living Body of our Lord and Savior, Jesus Christ."

Looking back now, I mark that night as an epiphany, the first of many moments when I saw the light of God's hope shine through the darkness. No doubt it's hard to be a Christian in America. But God is faithful. Just as the Holy Spirit raised up a Bonhoeffer in the midst of Nazi Germany, the same God used Bonhoeffer's words to name what I'd been looking for. In a letter

1. Dietrich Bonhoeffer, *Life Together* (New York: Harper and Row, 1954), 26.

to his brother in 1935, Bonhoeffer wrote, "The restoration of the church will surely come from a sort of new monasticism which has in common with the old only the uncompromising attitude of a life lived according to the Sermon on the Mount in the following of Christ."[2] At the margins of church and society, I started seeing signs of a new monasticism.

Falling into a River

Seven short years after that epiphany in Philadelphia, I got a call one afternoon from a reporter with *Time* magazine. "Could you describe for me the 'new monastic movement'?" he asked. It was a little strange to hear a reporter from a national magazine speak of our life in community as a "movement." "If new monasticism is a movement," I said, "it's much more like a river that we fell into than a march that we helped to organize." As I've looked around and listened to the stories of others over the past decade, it seems to me that God *is* moving in the American church, breathing life into Christ's body on the margins of society. But this is not a movement in which any of us are heroic organizers. It is, instead, something bigger than all of us—a movement that is *moving us* toward the kingdom of our God.

This is a book about what new monasticism has to say to the church in America, but I want to stress that new monasticism is about God's gift, not some idealists' dreams of peace and harmony in our time. This is easy to forget—especially when you're young like me (so maybe I'm just preaching to myself here). But Bonhoeffer is right again: "Whoever loves their dream of Christian community more than Christian community itself will become the destroyer of every Christian community, no matter how honest, earnest, and sacrificial their intentions may be."[3] If

2. Dietrich Bonhoeffer, *Testament to Freedom* (San Francisco: HarperSanFrancisco, 1997), 424.

3. Dietrich Bonhoeffer, *Gemeinsames Leben* (Gütersloh, Germany: Kaiser, 1997), 24. This is my translation of the German. For an English translation of Bonhoeffer's full text, see *Life Together*.

you don't believe that, all you need to do is live in community for a couple of years. Whenever life becomes about me and my ideals, community isn't possible. What is more, we forget the God who *is* community as Father, Son, and Holy Spirit.

This is why I worry about the "new" in new monasticism. We can't ignore how advertising and advanced capitalism have shaped us all to desire the next new thing and expect instant gratification. So it's worth saying for any of us who get jazzed up about new forms of Christian community that new monasticism ain't as new as it seems. I believe new monasticism is God's answer to the prayer of Dietrich Bonhoeffer, who, with so many others, saw the dawn of a post-Christian era in the twentieth century. But here's the part I love most: God started answering Bonhoeffer's prayer in Germany even before he prayed it.

Life in Germany after World War I was difficult for everyone. Most historians now agree that Germany's extreme poverty and social crisis in the 1920s generated the desperation that made Hitler possible. But at the same time that Bonhoeffer was beginning to study at the University of Berlin, God moved a group of Christians to leave Berlin for a village called Sannerz. Eberhard Arnold stated their goals succinctly:

> We want to be part of the stream of the Spirit that began at Pentecost. The first believers in Jerusalem distributed all their goods. "They were of one heart and soul, and shared all things in common." As soon as the Spirit was poured over them, nobody could hold onto property any longer.
>
> We want a genuine school of life, where the simplest work becomes a physical and artistic experience, where there is freedom from intellectualism and its pitfalls, where a new man can emerge, a creative man whose culture expresses what is real.
>
> We do not need theories or idealistic goals or prophets or leaders. We need brotherhood and sisterhood. We need to *live* Jesus' Sermon on the Mount. We need to show that a life of justice and forgiveness and unity is possible today.[4]

4. Eberhard Arnold, quoted in Peter Momsen, *Homage to a Broken Man* (Rifton, NY: Plough, 2004), 22.

The community called itself Bruderhof, "place of brother-hood." In the midst of a social crisis that would ultimately re-define Europe and make the United States the world's largest superpower, a few radical Christians carved out a space on the margins to live as God's holy people. More than two thousand guests came to visit the Bruderhof in its first year. Most of them did not stay, but a core community of people commit-ted themselves to God and one another. "It is not that we who stayed are good, and the others bad," Arnold's wife, Emmy, said. "It is just that they saw everything as an experiment, and we know it is a calling."[5] They had been called to shine as a light in Germany's darkest hour.

So as the Nazis began their program to "purify" Germany of undesirables, the Bruderhof continued to welcome gypsies and ex-cons, Marxists and Jews. When neighbors began to greet them with "Heil Hitler!" on the street, community members replied with a normal "Guten Morgen." Eberhard Arnold re-ceived warnings from friends in the government, but he insisted that the community should not leave Germany until forced to do so: "We must show with our lives what justice, love, and peace look like. We must give a witness that is indelibly branded in the books of history."[6] As Bonhoeffer was writing to his brother-in-law about "new monasticism," the Bruderhof was already living it in Hitler's Germany.

Meanwhile across the Atlantic, Americans were facing their own economic depression in the 1930s. As in Germany, radical movements in the United States sought alternatives to a way of life that didn't seem to be working. Nowhere did debates about radical politics rage more vigorously than in Greenwich Village, and that's where the young journalist Dorothy Day was when she found the Catholic Church. A convert to Christianity, Day brought with her questions about economic inequalities and social injustices. A friend suggested that she meet a French peasant named Peter Maurin who had been talking about the

5. Emmy Arnold, quoted in Momsen, *Homage to a Broken Man*, 37.
6. Eberhard Arnold, quoted in Momsen, *Homage to a Broken Man*, 93.

social teachings of the Catholic Church. Maurin spoke to Day about "a society where it is easier to be good," a vision for hospitality houses in the cities and agronomic universities in rural farmlands. On May 1, 1933, Day and Maurin began publishing this vision in *The Catholic Worker* newspaper.

Looking back years later, Day wrote, "We were just sitting there talking when Peter Maurin came in. We were just sitting there talking when lines of people began to form saying, 'We need bread.' We could not say, 'Go, be thou filled.' If there were six small loaves and a few fishes, we had to divide them. There was always bread."[7] People came asking where the social teachings of the Catholic Church were practiced, and Day welcomed them into her home. So as Bonhoeffer was writing *Life Together*, the Catholic Worker was born in America, a community of people who had received God's hospitality and were ready to offer it to others.

The same year Day and Maurin started publishing *The Catholic Worker* in New York, Clarence Jordan left the fields of Georgia, where he'd been born and raised, to study for the ministry at Southern Baptist Theological Seminary in Louisville, Kentucky. He had by that time already refused his military commission, telling his commanding officer that he could not serve both the Prince of Peace and the god of war. While studying the Bible in Louisville, he found himself drawn to people in excluded places. "I am seeing that the gospel of Jesus Christ has had its greatest growth when men have been dedicated enough to Him and His principles to quietly live them in the midst of dying and distressed humanity," he wrote to his mother. "Right now I'm inclined to revert to the simple but vital expression which Christianity had in its period of beginnings."[8]

Jordan studied the beginnings of Christianity carefully, completing his PhD in New Testament. In fall 1941, he read a letter by Martin England, published in a church journal, that outlined a vision for interracial communities in the South, intentionally

---

7. Dorothy Day, *The Long Loneliness* (New York: Harper and Row, 1952), 285.

8. Clarence Jordan, quoted in Charles Marsh, *The Beloved Community* (New York: Basic Books, 2005), 62.

organized on the model of the early church in Acts. Less than a year later, the Jordan and England families moved onto a piece of property in rural Georgia, determined to make it into a "demonstration plot for the Kingdom of God." Drawing on the New Testament Greek for "fellowship," they named their new community Koinonia Farm and set out to follow the way of Jesus in life together and daily work.

So twenty years before the era of what we generally refer to as the civil rights movement in America, some Christians in a forgotten corner of south Georgia began living together across racial lines, sharing what they had in common, and praying for the renewal of the church. A white Southern Baptist preacher, Jordan insisted that white Christians needed the black church to teach them who Jesus is. The Negro Christian, he said, "has an interpretation of Christ that the rest of the world needs."[9]

About the time Jordan returned to the fields of Georgia in search of authentic Christianity, John Perkins had an experience in the fields of rural Mississippi that would forever change his life. The son of bootleggers and sharecroppers, Perkins was a twelve-year-old black kid trying to make a dollar in the Jim Crow South. He took a job hauling hay for a white man, only to get paid fifteen cents at the end of a long day's work. "From that day on," Perkins says, "I began to understand something about the economic system and how it worked."[10]

Perkins's initial response was to get out of the South as fast as possible. By 1947 he'd made it to California and landed a job making ninety-eight cents an hour. In ten years of hard work, Perkins married, bought a home, secured a good job, and was proud to be providing for his family. He'd left God and church behind with the economic system of the South. "I was convinced that the Church—really the black Church, since that was the only one I knew anything about—was just

9. Marsh, *Beloved Community*, 65. I can't say in a sentence how important this point is. I have tried my best to say it in a book, *Free to Be Bound: Church Beyond the Color Line* (Colorado Springs: NavPress, 2008).

10. John Perkins, *Let Justice Roll Down* (Ventura, CA: Regal, 2006), 48.

one more kind of exploitation," he later wrote.[11] But Perkins's son came home from a Bible school one day talking about Jesus, and Perkins decided to go over to the Pentecostal church and see what they were teaching his son. He met Jesus in that church, and it wasn't long until Jesus called Perkins back to Mississippi.

In the throes of Mississippi's civil rights movement, Perkins learned to combine evangelical faith with grassroots political organizing and economic development. "Some thought we were civil-righters, others thought we were fanatical, others just thought we were 'some crazy niggers,' " Perkins recalls.[12] But after the civil rights movement had come and gone, Perkins kept working. Though he had been beaten nearly to death by white policemen in 1970, Perkins learned from Jesus about the power of love to overcome hatred. More than that, he learned that he couldn't embody God's love on his own. "I needed to build a community spirit. I needed to lean on people.... I was seeing more clearly than ever how important it is for Christians to be the people of God, and not just a collection of individual believers who gather weekly for the convenience of joint worship on Sunday."[13]

Perkins started preaching the "3 Rs" of Christian community development. First, he said, we have to relocate to neighborhoods that have been abandoned. What follows is redistribution of resources to correct for economic injustices. When people are together, sharing what they have so that no one goes without, true reconciliation can happen. Evangelicals around the country heard Perkins's plan and started putting it into action. White, black, Latino, and Asian Christians came together to form hundreds of organizations that now make up the Christian Community Development Association (CCDA). They live and work each day in the city neighborhoods where real estate agents won't take you. They are part of what Perkins calls "the quiet revolution."

11. Ibid., 63.
12. John Perkins quoted in Marsh, *Beloved Community*, 168.
13. Perkins, *Let Justice Roll Down*, 197.

Listening for the Quiet Revolution

The revolutions we read about in newspapers and history books aren't usually quiet. They're fueled by the power of military alliances or the "power of the people." The point of any revolution is to turn things around—to change the world that is into the world that ought to be. But the revolutions we hear about are the loud ones. The movements we hope for are ones that end in Washington.

But I think John Perkins is onto something: God has sown the seeds of a quiet revolution in abandoned inner-city neighborhoods and on our forgotten farmlands. Without any great fanfare, the Bruderhof, the Catholic Worker, Koinonia Farm, and CCDA have continued the subversive practices of loving one another, welcoming the stranger, sharing goods in common, and returning good for evil. As generations have grown old and died, leaving their work to others, the novelty of "the movement" has worn off. But the truth of it hasn't. The Sermon on the Mount isn't just an ideal vision for a new society. It is a sustainable way of life for those who live by faith.

When I was in high school, my brother and I started a landscaping business. We cut grass, trimmed weeds, sowed yards, and put in flowerbeds. During those hot summer days in North Carolina, I learned that some weeds are smarter than others. I don't remember what they're called, but some big suckers with a thick stem would grow up almost overnight. They could easily grow taller than me, mocking our efforts to keep yards looking nice. But those big, fast-growing weeds weren't very smart. They looked big and strong, but their roots were so short and shallow that I could pluck them out of the flowerbed with a single pull.

The weeds that I remember are the rhizomes. They were smart weeds, and I never could outwit them. Usually their stems were small, if they had any stems at all, and it was easy to whack them away with a Weed Eater. The next week, though, they would be back. Only there were *more* of them. I started trying to pull them up with my hands, but the stems would break off at the ground, just like when I whacked them with the Weed Eater. And the next week there would be more. I finally decided to read up on these little guys. That's when I learned that they're called "rhizomes" because they spread through an underground root structure, thriving beneath the surface and growing stronger all the time. There's really no way to get rid of them unless you tear up a whole yard. Fact of the matter is, they always win in the end.

Now, this is not a book about my adventures in landscaping, but those rhizomes did help me see something about how God moves in the world. The "quiet revolution" of God's kingdom doesn't spring up big and tall, parading its supremacy over all the other kingdoms of the earth. Instead, it spreads underground. It thrives beneath the surface. When you whack some little piece off, it just spreads somewhere else. And in the end, God's kingdom wins.

The new monasticism that sprang up in Germany in the early 1930s spread "beneath the surface" and sprouted in the United States among urban Catholics, rural Southern Baptists, and black evangelicals. Without much fanfare, it spread among Anabaptists who did alternative service in the 1950s. Historians who write about community movements in America often point to the Jesus People movement of the 1970s as the beginning of intentional Christian community, when thousands of young Christians had dramatic conversion experiences and hundreds of new communities were established. The same historians, however, generally note that the Jesus People were caught up in the idealism of the 1960s, which faded as the years wore on. Many gave up on their dreams to face reality, start families, and devote themselves to more conventional American Christianity. But this way of telling the story ignores the fact that there was already a "quiet revolution" in America long before the 1970s, and that some of those new communities from the seventies, like Jesus People USA (JPUSA) in Chicago, have continued to thrive by connecting with and learning from the tradition that preceded them. By God's grace they could see that they weren't starting something new, but that they had fallen into a river of faithfulness which flows on to join with other tributaries as it finds its way to the future God has given us.

Maybe everyone who finds Christian community chooses it because it offers something new. I know I did. When I met the people of the Simple Way in their early days of figuring out what God was doing with them, I saw something new happening there—something I had never seen before. It gave me hope that another world was possible and that the way of life Jesus taught and practiced could be a reality, right here on earth as it is in heaven. I was drawn in because I saw something new.

But I have stuck with Christian community because I believe it is part of something eternal—part of God's plan to redeem the world through a peculiar people. That's a story that goes all the way back to "in the beginning" and continues on in the lives of all who profess Jesus as Lord. In the context of that long story, it is possible to say that God is doing a "new" thing. But new in this case means eighty years old. And it doesn't mean a departure from God's movement in the past. New monasticism is a sign that God is still living and active, moving on the margins of the church to show us what faithfulness means in our time.

Following Jesus in a World at War

We live in a time marked by war. America's rise to the status of a world power was the direct result of World War II. For most of the latter half of the twentieth century we were deadlocked in a "cold war," amassing a nuclear arsenal with the power to extinguish all life on earth. The fall of the Soviet Union made America the "last remaining superpower," but this has not been an easy position to maintain. The attacks of September 11, 2001, are evidence that no amount of power can guarantee our safety. And we are now engaged in a "war on terror" that, if the words mean anything at all, is by definition a war without end. If the means of war are meant to terrify, how could war possibly end terror? Ours is an era of perpetual war.

What does it mean to follow the Prince of Peace—to be his body, even—in these times? In 2001, I married my friend, Leah, who had introduced me to the Simple Way, and we started trying to figure out how we were going to live our life together. We heard fellow Christians saying that God had called them to fight for regime change in Iraq and make the world safe for democracy, but we knew the church said this wasn't a "just war." Furthermore, we knew that Jesus said, "Love your enemies," but the U.S. government was calling young folks like us in the Army Reserves to go to Iraq and kill our enemies. Leah and I decided that it was time to follow our faith to its frightening conclusion. As Operation Iraqi Freedom began its Shock and Awe campaign against Iraq in March of 2003, we joined the Christian Peacemaker Teams in Baghdad as a ministry of presence against a war that the churches had called unjust.[14]

As our group was leaving Iraq in a caravan of three cars a couple of weeks later, the rear car hit a piece of shrapnel in the road and crashed into a side ditch. Those of us in the front two cars did not immediately realize what had happened, so our friends were left by the roadside in the middle of the desert, close to a town called Rutba. Seeing our friends in distress, a carful of Iraqis stopped, pulled them out of the ditch, and drove them into Rutba for medical assistance. When they found the doctor in town, he said to our friends, "Three days ago your country bombed our hospital. But whether you are American or Iraqi, Christian or Muslim, we will take care of you because we take care of everyone." He proceeded to sew up two bleeding heads and stabilize broken bones. One of our friends whom he bandaged up was Shane Claiborne from the Simple Way.

Shane says that our trip to Iraq helped him to see that the "family values" he learned growing up in the evangelical church extend not only to brothers and sisters on the streets but also to enemies in war zones. By the roadside near Rutba we relived the parable of the good Samaritan, learning about God's love

14. I have told the story of that trip and our conversion to Christian peacemaking in my book *To Baghdad and Beyond: How I Got Born Again in Babylon* (Eugene, OR: Cascade, 2005).

from the Iraqis who were supposed to be our nation's enemy (just as the Samaritans were supposed to be the enemies of the Jews to whom Jesus told the parable). We realized that we had been given the gift of community, even among enemies.

That gift at Rutba helped our vocational discernment. Returning to the United States, Leah and I knew what kind of life we were called to. We would start a Christian community of hospitality, peacemaking, and discipleship in an urban neighborhood of Durham, North Carolina, a city broken by a history of racial division and rapid economic change. There we would trust God to once again give us the gift of community. And we would call the community Rutba House.

Searching for St. Benedict

Starting a new community in a new town, Leah and I had lots of questions. We hadn't found all the answers, just a way in which we believed God would lead us forward. Community meant we were not alone. We had one another and a friend named Isaac Villegas who was willing to cast his lot with us in this new adventure. Thankfully, we had also met some of the people who had been seeking Christ in community since before we were born. Early in our time together, we received another gift: a grant to conduct a project that would enhance our ministry. Why not get some folks together to talk about this way of life that God has called us into? It was a simple proposal. We wanted to sit with friends and talk about the challenges we faced as followers of Jesus in America. We wanted to see if we could hear together what God was calling us to in Christian community.

When I made the proposal to my grant supervisor, he was very encouraging. "How many people are you thinking about inviting?" he asked. I said twenty or twenty-five. "Considering your resources," he said, "I'd invite ten." Six months later, more than sixty folks gathered in the sanctuary of St. John's Baptist Church, across the street from our house. In an article about the meeting, Mike Broadway and Isaac Villegas describe the scene:

> Academics rich with cultural capital sat beside others who professed a gospel committed to downward mobility. Wise elders and veterans of community formation and community development sat scattered among a large contingent of young adults who are part of fresh—even brash—experiments of faith. All had come together to pool their reflections on what to some appears to be an emerging trend, perhaps a movement, in the community of Christian churches in North America.[15]

We had called our meeting "The New Monasticism Gathering." Before we ever read Bonhoeffer's prayer, we had learned the phrase "new monasticism" from Leah's dad, Jonathan Wilson, who used it in a little book he wrote called *Living Faithfully in a Fragmented World*.[16] Jonathan had come across the idea of new monasticism by asking what the church could learn from the political philosopher Alasdair MacIntyre. MacIntyre has argued that traditions in the West are so fragmented that they have become unintelligible, even to insiders. If that is true, Jonathan said, then the church in the West must come to terms with the fact that fragmentation is a problem for us too. When we use a word like *gospel*, we often don't have a good sense of what it means. We've heard the word and know how to define it, but we can't quite make sense of what it looks like in practice—how we live it day to day.

Jonathan said that he had been haunted for some time by an enigmatic phrase he'd read in MacIntyre. "We are waiting not for a Godot," MacIntyre writes at the end of his book *After Virtue*, "but for another—and doubtless very different—St. Benedict."[17] What Jonathan hoped for when he wrote his

---

15. Michael Broadway and Isaac Villegas, "A New Monasticism," *Radix* 31, no. 4 (2005): 12.

16. Jonathan R. Wilson, *Living Faithfully in a Fragmented World* (Harrisburg, PA: Trinity, 1997).

17. Alasdair McIntyre, *After Virtue* (Notre Dame: University of Notre Dame Press, 1984), 263.

book was "not a new St. Benedict, but Christian communities that may produce a new St. Benedict."[18] He hoped God would move to create communities that could imagine new forms of faithfulness for American Christianity.

As we began to share our stories with one another, they began blending into a wonderful gift: the sketch of a new monastic movement in which all of us agreed that the Holy Spirit was at work. Despite differences, an incredible unity permeated the conversation among Catholics, Anabaptists, evangelicals, and mainline Protestants. That God is indeed doing a "new thing" in the North American church was the most definite conclusion of our days together.

In a culture of fear that is always at war, the good news that God is for us, shaping a quiet revolution, makes joy possible. "The glory of God," St. Irenaeus said, "is the human being fully alive."[19] Looking around the room at that first New Monasticism Gathering, I saw people who know good news—people who have found the "life that really is life" (1 Tim. 6:19). "Our journeys of faithfulness call us to hear the gospel again in a new light," Kent McDougal said after the gathering. "We are all deeply in need of hearing the gospel again."

It's true: we need to hear God's good news over and over again. We need to be reminded that God is *always* doing a new thing, always breathing new life into the church. If we have eyes to see, there are signs of something new right alongside the signs of the time. I close this chapter with the statement of hope and conviction that came out of our New Monasticism Gathering. It names the twelve marks that characterize new monastic communities. I like to think of it as a summary statement of the signs of hope we've seen.[20]

18. Wilson, *Living Faithfully*, 78.

19. Irenaeus of Lyon, *Adversus Haereses*, 4, 20, 7, in A. Roberts and J. Donaldson, ed., *The Ante-Nicene Fathers*, vol. 1 (Edinburgh: T. & T. Clark, 1989).

20. Each of these marks is considered in an essay by a member of a new monastic community in *School(s) for Conversion: Twelve Marks of a New Monasticism* (Eugene, OR: Cascade, 2005).

12 Marks of a New Monasticism ✳

Moved by God's Spirit in this time called America to assemble at St. Johns Baptist Church in Durham, NC, we wish to acknowledge a movement of radical rebirth, grounded in God's love and drawing on the rich tradition of Christian practices that have long formed disciples in the simple Way of Christ. This contemporary school for conversion, which we have called a "new monasticism," is producing a grassroots ecumenism and a prophetic witness within the North American church which is diverse in form, but characterized by the following marks:

1. Relocation to the abandoned places of Empire.
2. Sharing economic resources with fellow community members and the needy among us.
3. Humble submission to Christ's body, the church.
4. Geographical proximity to community members who share a common rule of life.
5. Hospitality to the stranger.
6. Nurturing common life among members of intentional community.
7. Peacemaking in the midst of violence and conflict resolution within communities along the lines of Matthew 18.
8. Lament for racial divisions within the church and our communities combined with the active pursuit of a just reconciliation.
9. Care for the plot of God's earth given to us along with support of our local economies.
10. Support for celibate singles alongside monogamous married couples and their children.
11. Intentional formation in the way of Christ and the rule of the community along the lines of the old novitiate.
12. Commitment to a disciplined contemplative life.

May God give us grace by the power of the Holy Spirit to discern rules for living that will help us embody these marks in our local contexts as signs of Christ's kingdom for the sake of God's world.

3

A VISION SO OLD IT LOOKS NEW

Peter Maurin of the Catholic Worker used to say that he believed in a vision for society that was "so old it looked like new." Maurin didn't think there was anything novel about Catholic Workers. They were just trying to remember what it meant to practice works of mercy, to follow the church's social teachings, to be God's peculiar people in the world. They were doing what Israel and the church had done for centuries, he thought. They were trying to live a vision so old that it looked like new.

I like Maurin's way of characterizing a movement that looked new to U.S. Christians in the 1930s. It seems he found a way both to receive the sign of Jonah as a gift and stay humble (something Jonah himself struggled with at Nineveh). Maurin said we can be encouraged by signs of something new precisely because they're signs of what God has been doing for centuries. But there's no room to be proud, no reason to think that God is doing something in our midst that hasn't been done before. I've already said that new monasticism ain't as new as it seems.

But I think Maurin said it better: it's really because it's so old that it looks new.

Of course, calling it monasticism is one way of reminding ourselves that this is an old vision. Monasticism goes back almost to the beginning of church history. In his book *The Monastic Impulse*, theologian Walter Capps summarizes the legacy of monastic history in a pretty strong statement. "Monasticism," he says, is the West's "most powerful and enduring instance of counter-culture."[1] I don't know about you, but when I think countercultural, I usually think punk rocker with a nose ring, not nun in a cloister. I've seen enough teenagers with long hair grow up to understand that what we usually call "counterculture" isn't very enduring. But I think this is a pretty incredible claim that Capps makes: not only does monasticism last longer but it is *more powerful* than any other form of resistance we've seen to mainstream society in the West. If that's true, then the real radicals aren't quoting Che Guevara or listening to Rage Against the Machine on their iPods. The true revolutionaries are learning to pray. If Capps is right, they always have been.

So while I'm no historian,[2] this chapter is an attempt to remember the monastic movements that have shaped the church and to note how they've offered alternatives to the pop culture of their day. I love these stories. But before I get excited and start telling them, I should offer one disclaimer: a lot of these stories are about the individuals for whom monastic movements were named. While I believe that God used these folks to do great things, I don't believe monastic movements are ever about one person. The *mon-* in monasticism points to one purpose (as in "singleness of heart"), not to one charismatic

---

1. Walter Capps, *The Monastic Impulse* (New York: Crossroad, 1983), 7.

2. This isn't just false humility. Almost everything I have to say in this chapter I learned from someone else. Unfortunately, I can't remember who taught me what most of the time. I do know, however, that Ivan Kauffman has helped me understand the context of the stories I'm telling. His book *Follow Me: The Intentional Christian in History* (Eugene, OR: Cascade, 2008) tells the story of monasticism in much more detail than I can here.

leader. The reason the church remembers these leaders is that, in one way or another, they embodied the hopes and longings of others. If I had time to tell their stories in more detail, it would be easier to see how their lives were dependent on others. But since I have to hurry to get two thousand years of church history in one chapter, this little disclaimer from the get-go will have to do.

As long as I'm making disclaimers, it seems that another is in order. The story I tell here is, for the most part, the story of the dominant church in the West. By telling the monastic version of this story, I hope to show both how far we've strayed from the gospel at times and how God has moved to remind us of our true calling. It is both a tragic and a hopeful story, and it seems to me that for better or worse we have to own it as Christians in the United States. But it must be said that ours is not the only story. Nor does it seem that our story has necessarily produced the most faithful members in the great communion of saints. Jesus sent the first disciples to proclaim his kingdom in all the earth. So the church has a history in the Middle East, in Asia, in Africa, and in South America. We need to learn those stories too and to remember that they are part of our story. A global sense of church history helps us see that while new monasticism may be one way God is moving in our world, it's certainly not the only way. If anything, new monasticism ought to make clear that the United States is not the epicenter of Christianity in our world.

Antony and the First Monastics

When we think about the early church, we often think about how Christians were a persecuted minority, eaten by lions and burned at the stake by Roman emperors. Even though that kind of persecution was not constant for the early church, it is true that it cost a lot to follow Jesus for most of Christianity's first three centuries. But by the mid-third century, Christianity had spread to people in power—Roman citizens who had money and were in with the emperor. About then, the world started changing for Christians. Of course, no one complained about not having to worry about the police knocking the door down in the middle of a worship service. But some Christians were concerned that believers would forget the cost of discipleship.

In the midst of this transition, an eighteen-year-old Egyptian Christian named Antony lost both of his parents and suddenly became responsible for his family's household. His parents had been well-to-do, which meant he was responsible for a sizable amount of capital in a city where most of the population was poor. This economic situation troubled Antony to the point that in AD 251, after hearing Jesus's command to "sell what you have and give it to the poor," he gave his parents' land to their neighbors and sold all their possessions. After he'd given all the money away, Antony started trying to figure out what God wanted him to do with his life.

At that time in Egypt there was the occasional hermit who devoted himself to prayer and fasting. One of these holy men lived in the village next to Antony's, and his biographer says Antony "emulated him in goodness."[3] Antony made the rounds from one hermit to the next, learning the disciplines of a godly life and developing quite a reputation for holiness, even among his peers. But then something happened to Antony. He started to lose his resolve, to remember the life he'd left behind, and to wonder if he was really getting anywhere. When he tried to sleep at night, Antony dreamed of lavish meals and seductive women. He said his mind was filled with "a great dust cloud of considerations." But he continued the prayer and fasting that his mentors had taught him. Antony cried out to God for help. Then one day he heard a human voice speaking to him. He asked who it was, and the voice answered that he was "the friend of fornication." Antony saw a small, dark demon and listened to him complain about how Antony had resisted all of

---

3. We know Antony's story because Athanasius, bishop of Alexandria, visited him and wrote a "Life of Antony." This quote and all others taken from Athanasius, *Athanasius: The Life of Antony and the Letter to Marcellinus*, trans. Robert Gregg, Classics of Western Spirituality (Mahwah, NJ: Paulist, 1980), 32.

his schemes. "From now on," Antony said to him, "you cause me no anxiety, for the Lord is my helper, and I shall look upon my enemies."[4] When he said this, the demon fled.

Antony's experience with the demon opened his eyes to the spiritual battle that was going on in the third-century world. The devil, he saw, was using the power and favors of the Roman Empire to entice Christians. Though at first they had just seemed like a "dust cloud," Antony realized that these forces were at work in his life and he didn't have the power to understand them, even less to resist. But if God was his helper, Antony knew he could face the devil and his schemes head on. He could fight on the Lord's side in the battle against evil. And he could do it best, Antony decided, by going out into the desert.

"Nearly twenty years he spent in this manner, pursuing the ascetic life by himself," Athanasius says. But somehow word spread about this holy man who'd gone off to do battle with the devil. After twenty years, some of his friends went to find him. They tore down the door of his hermitage and asked Antony to come back to the city with them. Antony agreed, and when he came back to the city he brought the power of God with him. "Through him the Lord healed many of those present who suffered from bodily ailments; others he purged of demons, and to Antony he gave grace in speech. Thus he consoled many who mourned, and others hostile to each other he reconciled in friendship, urging everyone to prefer nothing in the world above the love of Christ."[5] A revival like no one had ever seen swept through the Egyptian church, with a power to change lives and renew broken relationships. All the bishops of the church couldn't have organized such a movement. But the witness of Antony, who trusted the Lord and fought the devil face to face, literally moved thousands to give themselves over to the way of Jesus. "And so, from then on, there were monasteries in the mountains," Athanasius says, "and the desert was made

4. Ibid., 35.
5. Ibid., 42.

a city by the monks, who left their own people and registered themselves for the citizenship in the heavens."[6]

So monasticism was born. During a time when Christianity was transitioning from the persecuted faith of a minority to the state-sponsored religion of the powerful, the monastic impulse drove desert abbas (fathers) and ammas (mothers) out into the abandoned places to learn God's power by fighting the devil face to face. They helped the church discover new forms of faithfulness for a new time. But even more than that, they set a precedent for how the church remembers the power of God when the powers of this world are in transition. They introduced the monastic impulse to relocate and reimagine our role from the margins of society.

Benedict and a "School for the Lord's Service"

By the end of the fourth century, it was clear that the imperial project of Rome had failed. Caesar Augustus had brought the whole Mediterranean world under Rome's power, but the Romans had not been able to figure out a way of life that was sustainable for all those diverse peoples. The sack of Rome by the Visigoths was more traumatic for Romans than September 11, 2001, was for us in the United States. Afterward there were no illusions that life could go on as before. Europe was in the midst of a social crisis.

At the beginning of the fifth century Augustine of Hippo wrote *The City of God* to argue that Rome had fallen because it was built on the worship of false gods. Christians could go on living in the ruins of the Empire, Augustine said, because they were citizens of another city, a people on their way to God's kingdom. As it turned out, Augustine not only had his theology right, but also described well what would happen throughout the fifth century. Christian communities sheltered people from the economic fallout of a crumbling empire and

6. Ibid., 42–43.

offered the hope of a different kingdom, "on earth as it is in heaven."

This is the situation that Benedict of Nursia was born into. Though he is now remembered as the father of Western monasticism, we don't know very much about Benedict's life. We wouldn't know anything at all except for the fact that a fellow named Gregory, who became a monk at a monastery that Benedict started in Rome, went on to become Pope Gregory the Great. He wrote a biography of Benedict and, more important, held up Benedict's *Rule* as a model for community life. After that, new monastic communities spread across all of Europe.

In his *Rule*, Benedict said that monastic community is to be a "school for the Lord's service."[7] In the midst of society, as people struggled to get by in the world, Benedictine communities were to be islands where people could learn a different way of doing life. That way of living was summarized in the Latin phrase *ora et labora*—"to pray and to work." Benedict's *Rule* offered a model for communities where people could live a life of prayer together, serving one another and the community around them. They would, as Gandhi later said, "be the change they seek" in the world. And through the practice of hospitality, they would welcome others into their life with God.

In our democratic world of supposedly endless possibility, it's hard to imagine the radical alternative that Benedict offered people in the so-called Dark Ages. In early European society, there was little to no social mobility. Peasants had children who grew up to be peasants. People with power passed it down to their children. There was no such thing as a middle class. The one long shot at possibly moving up from the lower classes was the military, and this option was available only to men.

But all of this changed when monastic communities started popping up. Benedictine life was literally an alternative society. Rich and poor were treated as equals under the *Rule*, serving one another out of reverence for Christ. What is more, women could choose not to remain in their father's house or marry

7. Prologue to *Rule of Benedict* (Garden City, NY: Image, 1975).

into another man's house but to share life and even have the possibility of leadership positions in a house of sisters. These little societies within society became like leaven in a lump of dough, creating pockets of freedom where people could imagine alternatives to the violence and grinding poverty of the world around them. As leaven tends to do, these communities spread among the peoples they touched.

Francis, Clare, and the Cash Economy

Even though Benedictine communities spread far and wide in Europe, they didn't transform it into the kingdom of God once and for all. Unfortunately, the story of Benedictines in Europe in many ways parallels the story of the church in its first few centuries. As more and more people recognized the value of these communities, they were offered favors by people in power and often forgot the peculiar power of God. Hospitality changed from hosting Christ in the poor to hosting nobility in hopes of a larger endowment. As Christine Pohl has noted, "Wealthy monastic houses provided important guests with fine quarters and lavish fare, offering a standard of entertainment that was highly regarded. . . . Thus, monastic hospitality in the Middle Ages generally reinforced social boundaries, a clear departure from the vision of the early writers."[8] In short, monasticism strayed far from its roots and lost the power of its witness.

In the eleventh century, Europe began to undergo another serious transition. Improved agriculture (due in part to Benedictine influence) produced more food, which in turn led to dramatic population growth. More people meant more laborers who were employed not only in agriculture but also in developing industries like cloth production. This led to a concentration of people in towns, where they no longer lived off the fruit of their labors as they had on the land but rather were paid in

8. Christine Pohl, *Making Room: Recovering Hospitality as a Christian Tradition* (Grand Rapids: Eerdmans, 1999), 48.

currency. And when people had money—well, they spent it. They bought and sold things in stores that were financed by banks and owned by merchants. Historians sometimes call this the rise of the "money economy," not so much because there had never been currency before but rather because it had never so defined the way people lived. In this new era, money was power.

Benedictine monks, of course, took vows of poverty, but that poverty had for centuries meant giving up their claims to military might and political position. Under the *Rule*, monastic communities still built big buildings and owned land (lots of it, as a matter of fact). And with an increased demand for space in Europe and the advent of a money economy, it turned out the monks were actually rich. As Jesus once said, "It is easier for a camel to go through the eye of a needle than for someone who is rich to enter the kingdom of God" (Mark 10:25). Great wealth made it hard for even the monks to follow Jesus.

Toward the end of the twelfth century, when this transition to a money economy was well under way, Francis Bernardone was born to a cloth merchant in the Italian town of Assisi. For most of his youth Francis lived a very self-indulgent life. He dreamed of being a knight but was a failure in battle and spent a year as a prisoner of war. After recovering from a sickness that he caught in prison, Francis tried once again to be a soldier. But during his first night in the military camp, he had a vision in which God asked him whether it was better to serve the Lord or his vassal. Francis decided he was called to serve the King of kings and promptly left his post with the army.

Francis's dream of being a knight in the Lord's service led him to a number of economic experiments, which mostly entailed giving his father's money away to the poor or selling his father's cloth to rebuild a dilapidated church building. In 1208 Francis heard a Gospel reading in church: "Take no gold, or silver, or copper in your belts, no bag for your journey, or two tunics, or sandals, or a staff; for laborers deserve their food" (Matt. 10:9–10). Hearing those instructions from his Lord,

Francis renounced his father's wealth. In front of the whole town and the bishop, Francis stripped naked, returning even the clothes off his back to his father, and said that from then on he would rely on "our Father, who art in heaven."

Thus began a new monastic movement in Europe. Kelly Johnson sums up well the contribution that Francis made: "Francis's poverty, from the beginning, was about publicly calling for gifts which reveal Christ's church. The metaphor of religious life had shifted from a renunciation of war that witnesses to Christ's peace toward a renunciation of profit-taking that witnesses to Christ's plenty."[9] In the face of the new money economy, Francis said that brothers who wanted to walk with him could work for food or beg alms, but under no circumstances were they to accept money. They couldn't even touch it. Traveling on foot from city to city, they were to proclaim and perform the good news of God's abundance. Money's power worked to convince people that scarcity is the fundamental economic reality. But Francis insisted on a deeper truth—that his Father who fed the sparrows and clothed the lilies of the field would take care of him.

Two years after Francis abandoned himself to God's abundance, the pope approved an order for twelve Friars Minor to follow Jesus according to the rule that Francis had written. Ten years later there were five thousand friars in Europe. This new monasticism spread like wildfire as rich and poor together begged to the glory of God.

On Palm Sunday, 1212, in Assisi, just a few years after the Friars Minor were established, a young woman named Clare sneaked away from her family one night to meet Francis, saying that she wanted to marry Christ in poverty. He shaved her head, gave her a peasant's robe to wear, and delivered her to a Benedictine women's community. But when her family came looking for Clare, the Benedictine sisters asked Francis to find somewhere else for her. He moved Clare into a church he had

9. Kelly Johnson, *The Fear of Beggars: Stewardship and Poverty in Christian Ethics* (Grand Rapids: Eerdmans, 2007), 32.

rebuilt at San Damiano, which would become home to another order, the Poor Clares. Francis and Clare, like Benedict and Scholastica (the founder of Benedictine women's communities), responded to the monastic impulse in their time, giving rise to movements they couldn't have imagined beforehand. They remind us that new monasticism is a gift God gives to the church, especially during times of transition when it's difficult to find our way. Who knows where Christianity would be without Francis and Clare? All I can say for sure is that they were a great gift to the church of the thirteenth century. And they're a gift to us—especially when we pay attention to their witness in its context.

Protestant Monasticism

It's no secret that the sixteenth-century church in Europe was again in serious need of reform. Though it wasn't happening everywhere, there really were people selling salvation as if it were a commodity. (If you think this was just a sixteenth-century problem, try watching a little late-night Christian TV.) Protestants like me often look back to Martin Luther as the herald of true Christian faith to a church that had become corrupt, and there is some truth to that. But we easily forget that Martin Luther was an Augustinian monk who learned the gospel he preached from his confessor in a monastery. We forget that much of the so-called Protestant Reformation was driven by the monastic impulse.

Nowhere is this clearer than in the Radical Reformation. After Luther's ninety-five theses stirred up popular disagreement with some of the doctrine and practices of the Catholic Church, some political rulers in Germany found it advantageous to declare their territory Protestant, take control of the church's coffers and landholdings in their jurisdiction, and expand their rule in the name of religious difference. In this way, Catholic and Protestant churches were equally state-sponsored institutions. But the Radical Reformation emerged when people within this tumultuous environment insisted that church was really about allegiance to Jesus, not to a Protestant or Catholic ruler.

One such group gathered for prayer in Zurich on the evening of January 21, 1525. George Blaurock later described their experience this way:

> And it came to pass that they were together until fear began to come over them, yea, they were oppressed within their hearts. Thereupon, they began to bow their knees to the Most High God in heaven and called upon him. . . . For flesh and blood and human forwardness did not drive them, since they well knew what they would have to bear and suffer on account of it. After the prayer, George Cajacob arose and asked Conrad to baptize him for the sake of God, with the true Christian baptism upon his faith and knowledge. And when he knelt down with that request and desire, Conrad baptized him, since at that time there was no ordained minister to perform such work. After that was done, others similarly desired George to baptize them, which he also did upon their request. Thus they together gave themselves to the Lord.[10]

It's important to note that this rebaptism was ultimately about allegiance. In the so-called Christian culture of sixteenth-century Europe, where infants were baptized into church and state citizenship at the same time, the monastic impulse drove some Christians to "give themselves to the Lord" by choosing to go once more under the baptismal waters. For this they were called Anabaptists (rebaptizers). At a time when Catholics and Protestants could agree on almost nothing else, they agreed that it was best to kill these Radical Reformers.

Michael Sattler was one of the Anabaptists who counted the cost and chose a path that would lead to martyrdom. For Sattler, that journey started at St. Peter's in the Black Forest, a Benedictine monastery. There he helped lead a reform movement in the early sixteenth century, calling the brothers to return

---

10. George Hunston Williams, *The Radical Reformation*, 3rd ed. (Kirksville, MO: Sixteenth Century Journal Publications, 1992), 217.

to the true spirit of Benedict's *Rule*. But Sattler was ultimately dissatisfied with the brothers and left the monastery in search of a new community. He found this among the Anabaptists and cast his lot with them.

Though he survived for only a few years, Sattler was the main author of the Schleitheim Articles, a statement of the Radical Reformation's vision around which numerous independent groups rallied. A biography of Sattler by C. Arnold Snyder notes the parallels between the Schleitheim Articles and Benedict's *Rule*. What these radicals were calling for, he observes, was voluntary membership in community, a common way of life, the disciplined pursuit of holiness, and leaders elected by the community. In other words, they wanted a church that looked like Benedict's monastery.[11]

Though Protestants haven't called their reform movements "monastic," it's worth noting that this impulse has continued through the past five centuries, giving rise to Quakers, Shakers, and all sorts of other radical Christian groups. I'm convinced that the most significant new monastic movement in the United States was the slave church that arose from the "hush harbors" of plantations in the so-called Christian South. In the face of a white Christianity that justified the ownership of black people, black Christians founded an underground community in which holiness was stressed, citizenship in heaven defined allegiance, economic sharing and hospitality were practiced, and church was understood to be "first family," where God alone is Father. For years scholars said little could be known about the theology and practice of slave churches because there were no historical documents. But thankfully Albert J. Raboteau recognized that the theology of the slave church was in its songs, and the practices of its members were recorded in the personal narratives of emancipated slaves from the late nineteenth century. His book *Slave Religion* is a crucial contribution to the history of the church in America. I often tell people that I know the

11. C. Arnold Snyder, *The Life and Thought of Michael Sattler* (Scottsdale, PA: Herald, 1984), 185. I owe my friend Weldon Nisly credit for making me aware of the Benedictine roots of the Anabaptist vision.

black church was born of the monastic impulse because the folks at our church in Walltown call one another brother and sister, just like they always have in monasteries.

Getting Back to Our Roots

Telling the story of monasticism in a single chapter, I feel like the author of Hebrews, who came to the end of the roll call of faith in chapter 11 and asked, "What more should I say? For time would fail me to tell of . . ." (Heb. 11:32). I don't have time to write about Julian of Norwich, St. Patrick, Catherine of Siena, John of the Cross, Teresa of Ávila, Ignatius of Loyola, Mother Teresa, the Waldensians, the Brethren of the Common Life, the Pietists, or the Puritans, just to name a few. I do hope, however, that by putting a few of monasticism's best-known stories into context, we can begin to get a sense of the story we find ourselves in. In the history of the church, it's nothing new to look around and find our institutions severely compromised. Ours is a tragic story.

But it is also a story of hope. In every era God has raised up new monastics to pledge their allegiance to God alone and remind the church of its true vocation. These people have not been perfect. Like the apostle Paul, they often considered themselves "chief among sinners." But one way or another, they found hope in the story of the people of God and strove to get back to the roots of that story. For this they were often called radicals (*radix* is Latin for "root"). Sometimes they were even killed. But they knew the life they found in Christ was worth more than anything else this world could offer.

These saints who've called us back to our roots generation after generation remind us that the roots of God's kingdom are rhizomes. They spread beneath the surface, effecting change from below. It is a quiet revolution—one that is often ignored by the newspapers and missed by the historians. But it is, in the end, how God plans to save the world. Like those rhizomes, God's kingdom just won't go away. As the book of

Daniel says, it "became a great mountain and filled the whole earth" (Dan. 2:35).

Since I started this chapter with Peter Maurin's notion of a "vision so old it looks like new," it's fitting to end with Dorothy Day's conviction about how God's kingdom grows from the bottom up. In his biography of Day, Robert Coles writes about how she understood working from the bottom to be "Christ's technique." "She was always taking Jesus as seriously as possible," Coles observes. "She was always trying to remember that He was an obscure carpenter who in His early thirties, did not go talk with emperors and kings and important officials, but with equally obscure people, and thereby persuaded a few fishermen, a few farm people, a few ailing and hard-pressed men and women, that there was reason for them to have great hope."[12]

Such radical hope is the heart of the monastic impulse, always calling the church back to its roots underground. If such a vision seems novel, it may be a sign of how far we've strayed from our story. This is why the first task of any monastic movement is to remind the church that our story is the adventure of God's relationship with a peculiar people. But that story deserves a chapter of its own.

12. Robert Coles, *Dorothy Day: A Radical Devotion* (Reading, MA: Perseus, 1987), 90.

4

GOD'S PLAN TO SAVE THE WORLD THROUGH A PEOPLE

I should have known better, but I grew up thinking that the Bible was mostly about how I could have a relationship with God and become a good person. I say I should have known better because the people who raised me up in the church made me memorize the King James Version of the Bible. And in the KJV, when the Bible is talking to you, it almost always says "ye." "Be *ye* fruitful, and multiply," God says in Genesis (9:7). "*Ye* are the light of the world," Jesus teaches in Matthew (5:14). In the verses I grew up memorizing, almost all the you's were ye's.

Somehow this didn't sink in for me until I learned the grammar of the Bible. (They make you do that when you study Hebrew and Greek.) I can't say that I mastered the biblical languages, but in college I did have a Greek professor who was from Oklahoma and hadn't been corrupted at all by academic pretension. As they say here in our neighborhood, he knew how to "make it plain." My professor liked to say that most of

the you's in scripture are ya'lls. That is, almost all of the second-
person pronouns are *plural* in the New Testament Greek. Same
is true with the Hebrew. It's "ye," not "thou," "ya'll," not "you."
The Bible isn't addressed to a person but to a people.

Now I don't usually get very excited about grammar lessons,
and I'll admit that this is a pretty simple one. But in the context of new monastic community, the fact that the Bible isn't
addressed to "you" but to "ya'll" has changed the way I read
scripture. Like I said before, I used to believe the Bible was
mostly an instruction manual for how to get right with God
and be a good person. And I wasn't all wrong. The God of the
Bible does want to have a relationship with me. And people who
know God do become better people. But if the Bible is a story
about God's plan to save the world *through a people*, then my
salvation and sanctification depend on finding my true home
with God's people. Apart from the story of this people, I can't
have a relationship with God. Without the church, there's no
chance of becoming holy.

My friend Tim Otto from the Church of the Sojourners community in San Francisco likes to make this point with a little
thought experiment. Imagine, he says, that you and your friends
have never played basketball. You've heard of basketball. You
know that other people play the game. But you've never played
basketball yourself. Then one day when you're out with your
friends, you come upon a basketball court. Someone says, "Why
don't we play?" But you don't know how to play. Then someone
else says, "Wait! There's a library across the street. I'll go grab
a rulebook and we'll learn how to play."

Well, imagine that your friend runs into the library to grab
a book on basketball, but in his haste he checks out a book on
soccer. (OK, OK, I know it's a stretch, but use your imagination.) He comes back to the court and starts teaching everyone
the rules. "We need one round ball." OK. "We need a playing
field with boundaries." Got it. "We need to split up into two
different teams and try to shoot the ball into goals that are on
opposite ends of the playing field." So far so good. It looks like
this soccer manual might work all right.

The only problem is that when you start playing, you realize it's extremely difficult to kick a soccer ball through a basketball hoop. Not that it's impossible—every once in a while somebody might get it through. But it's an incredibly frustrating game. You begin to wonder if your friend misinterpreted the manual. Or maybe, you think, the rulebook was no good to start with. At any rate, you'd hope at some point the whole group could stop and ask whether you were even playing the right game.

Often we read scripture as if it were a soccer manual telling us how to play basketball. That's why a lot of Christians in America wonder whether they're playing the right game. At first we accused others of misinterpreting the Bible. Then some of us began to doubt whether the Bible was even a good book. But at some point we have to ask whether we've been playing the wrong game. What game does the Bible gives us instructions for anyway?

For much of the church, the game we try to play could be called "Make Myself." The Bible is a long and complicated collection of stories that we need to boil down to principles, this game says. When you get to the point of all those stories, they're really about how to make myself. The Bible tells me how to make myself good, make myself rich, make myself kind, or make myself humble. We might argue about just what the Bible calls me to make myself. But most of the church agrees that this is the point of the game. Of course, I cannot make myself all alone. To be all that I can be, I need Jesus. But in this game called Make Myself, the Bible is all about what Jesus wants me to do to make myself what I ought to be.

There's another version of this game that is very similar. It could be called "Make Yourself." In this game I know that the Bible isn't just for me. It also tells me how other people should live. So I say to my neighbor, "Make yourself loving." And I say to my nation, "Make yourself just." I say to the rich, "Make yourself compassionate." And I say to the powerful, "Make yourself humble." The great thing about Make Yourself is that you can play it while you're playing Make Myself. People do both all the time.

The trouble is that the Bible doesn't quite work as a manual for either of these games. Almost, but not quite. Sort of like trying to play basketball with a soccer manual. Lots of things seem to work out at first. Abraham seems like a pretty good example of someone who made himself faithful. The prophets give us pretty good ammunition for the next round of Make Yourself. But the more you try to get inside the story of the Bible, the more it feels like it was written for a different game.

I think new monastic communities point to the fact that the Bible is really about a game called "God Makes a People." This is the game the Bible was written to teach us to play—because it's the game we were made for. I guess there are lots of ways you could try to test and see if God's making of a people is really what the Bible is about. Historians could tell us whether other people have tried to read it this way before. Textual scholars could tell us whether there's anything in the Bible that suggests we should read it this way. Sociologists might tell us what difference it makes to read the Bible as a story about God forming a people. But it seems to me that if you wanted to know whether a soccer manual was really meant to help you play soccer, the best you could do would be to try to play a game of soccer, informed by what you find in the manual.

Best I can figure, this is what new monastic communities are trying to do in the church today. We're living together as God's people to see how the Bible works as a manual for how to live together as God's people. This chapter is about how we're learning to read scripture together and what it's teaching us in community.

In the Beginning

The Bible begins with a story about how God created the heavens and the earth and hovered over the waters in the darkness of a new world. When God speaks, light shines on the waters. Then God speaks again and says, "Let there be a dome in the midst of the waters, and let it separate the waters from the waters" (Gen. 1:6). God carves out a space for life to exist. In between the waters, he makes a home. The Bible begins with a story about our God, the Homemaker.

In the course of five days God creates a great number of things. John's Gospel summarizes it like this: "All things came into being through him, and without him not one thing came into being" (John 1:3). Our Homemaker fills the earth with all sorts of good things and then pauses to say, "Let us make humankind in our image" (Gen. 1:26). Christians have often noted how God speaks of himself (I mean, *their selves*) in the plural here. Since we believe God exists as Father, Son, and Holy Spirit, this sort of internal conversation makes sense to the church. But we shouldn't forget that the verse is as much about humanity as it is about God. The God who is three persons in community creates humanity in the image of community. We could translate verse 27 like this: "In the image of God he created [the human being]; male and female he created them."

So the home God creates here on earth is a house of hospitality. Father, Son, and Spirit love one another so much that they want to invite others into that love. They create a space where they can share life with people created in their image. It's a pretty incredible image of what the world was meant to be. God wanted a place to live together with people, so he built a home out of nothing and created a people. Then God told them how they could live the good life with him.

But those very first people weren't satisfied just knowing the good life with God. They wanted to know the good and the evil. Each wanted to choose individually what they thought would be best for them. You might say they started trying to play Make Myself. But that wasn't the game they'd been made for. No sooner had they started trying to play it than they realized they were naked, out of place, and alienated from God. They hid themselves from one another with leaves and hid behind a tree from God. Knowing good and evil, it was hard to trust others. This made life together unimaginable.

But violence was what made life together *impossible*. By the second generation of human history, Cain had killed his brother and left his home, fearing that someone else would take his life. People could not live together in peace after one person had killed another. God decided this was so far from the plan he'd had for life together with people that it would be better to destroy them all with a flood of water. But once again God chose to carve out a space between the waters where life could flourish. He told Noah to build an ark and invite in two animals of every kind, along with his family. In that new home, Noah's family would learn how to live together with God in the world.

Unfortunately, these people didn't turn out much better than the first. No sooner had the ark landed on dry land than Noah planted a vineyard, harvested grapes, and made some wine. Like Adam back in the garden, Noah was naked as he enjoyed the fruit of his labor. But he got a little drunk and was still uncovered when one of his sons came by to see him. Whatever Noah might have thought at first, he and his family evidently had not restored the trust that existed between people in Eden. Noah and his son had it out when he sobered up, and Noah ended up cursing his son.

The next story the Bible tells is about how Noah's descendants spread out all over the earth. Even though they lived in different places, they all spoke one language. But when they came to a plain called Shinar, some people got together and decided they would build a tower all the way to heaven. They didn't want to be scattered out like people had been ever since Cain killed Abel. They wanted to be together in community. And they were determined to make it happen. But God looked down and saw how people were about to destroy themselves by trying to be together with violence in their hearts. So the Bible says God confused the people's language at Babel. "The LORD scattered them abroad from there over the face of all the earth," Genesis says, "and they left off building the city" (11:8). Up until then everyone had been part of one people, speaking the same language. But from then on there were many peoples. Babel is the beginning of multiculturalism. From then on one people checked another people's power lest all humanity destroy itself.

Immediately after this story about where the peoples of the earth come from, we find the story of how God called Abram. "I will make of you a great nation, and I will bless you," God says to Abram. "I will bless those who bless you, and the one who curses you I will curse; and in you all the families of the earth shall be blessed" (Gen. 12:2–3). In a world full of peoples who fear one another and fight for power among themselves, God chooses one people to be his own. This is God's plan to save the world through a people. Like Adam and Noah before him, Abram hears God's voice. It is the voice of love, calling him into community. "I will make of you a great nation," God says. Abram's children will become a people who live together with God in the world. And when other peoples see how good it is to live together with their Maker, they will want to come and be part of God's people too. Through this one people, all the peoples of the world will be blessed.

What a People Needs

Well, I started by saying this was a chapter about reading the Bible in community, but so far we've just read Genesis—and less than half of it. But at this point we can pick up the pace a little bit. The first five books of the Old Testament are what Israel called Torah—that is, the Law. Most Christians in America don't like the biblical law. To us it seems like a bunch of old rules that don't make much sense anymore. (Why shouldn't you be able to eat a goat that was boiled in its mother's milk?) At best we figure God gave us the law to teach us that we could never be good enough on our own and that we all need grace. But if that's all the law was for, we don't really need it anymore. This is why you don't hear many sermons on Leviticus.

But if the Bible really is about God forming a people, then we need the law. We need it because every people needs laws. Laws delineate how a people is going to live together. When the people of Israel came out of the domination system of Egypt, God gave them his law so they could know another way to live together. In Deuteronomy, God says that the law is life: "I call heaven and earth to witness against you today that I have set before you life and death. . . . Choose life so that you and your descendants may live" (30:19). God wanted Israel to show the whole world what it looks like to really live.

If you live in community for a while, the Ten Commandments start to make a lot of sense. Take for example the commandment not to kill. I've lived with other people long enough to know that violence can be a real temptation. But killing a fellow community member would really mess up the dynamics in a household. So it's good that God gave us a law against killing. I'm glad we can agree that's not an option in community. Likewise with adultery, stealing, and lying. It's just hard to live with people if they're sleeping with your spouse, stealing your car, or lying to you. I'm glad God told us, "Thou shalt not" do that stuff.

It's pretty easy to see how some laws in the Old Testament are for the community's good. But why does a people need to keep Sabbath, avoid idols, and eat kosher? Most of the commandments in Torah are about purity or holiness. What does that have to do with life together? The Church of the Sojourners, where my aforementioned friend Tim lives, is a new monastic community in the Mission District of San Francisco. They've learned a lot about what it means to be a people in their twenty years together. When they came together as a community in the mid-1980's, they got serious about the "shalts" and "shalt nots" of Scripture. They knew God didn't want them to kill, steal, or lie. They had also begun to suspect that God didn't want them to live for themselves, hoard their wealth, or forget the needy in their city. Instead, they heard God commanding them in scripture to serve the poor, welcome the stranger, feed the hungry, and love one another. They avoided the "shalt nots" and gave themselves to God's "shalts," working hard at them. Doing this together felt like real life.

But San Francisco is a pretty progressive place. People live together there for all kinds of reasons, talk a lot about love, and welcome most anyone. After Church of the Sojourners had been living together in San Francisco for a while, one of their pastors, Jack Bernard, decided to make everyone in the community a wooden cross. He told them they should wear it around their neck all the time as a reminder that God had set them apart to be a holy people. Tim, who works as a nurse at San Francisco General Hospital, started wearing his wooden cross on the AIDS ward. In a place where many people had come out as homosexual, Tim says it was a powerful experience to "come out" as a Christian. His cross was a constant reminder that he was part of a people who were living as sojourners in San Francisco. Jack's crosses reminded Sojourners that they are a people set apart.

God gave the law to Israel not only to show them a way to live but also to remind them that they were a people set apart. If we read the history books of the Old Testament, they're full of stories about how God's people forgot who they were, wandered off, and started following other gods. When they did, they inevitably left behind the good and just way of life that God had given them as a gift. The book of Judges ends by saying, "In those days there was no king in Israel, all the people did what was right in their own eyes" (21:25). A law unto themselves, the people forgot their good life with God.

But God didn't abandon his people. He sent them priests and kings and prophets to remind them who they were. Priests were set aside to lead God's people in sacrifices and celebrations, worshiping God as their full-time work. Those 150 psalms in the middle of our Bibles make up Israel's songbook, an important reminder that God's people have a liturgical life where they sing, pray, celebrate, and lament together. Even though Israel had lots of bad kings, the good kings remembered God's law and led the people in righteousness. And the prophets—well, they were a constant thorn in the side of bad kings, corrupt priests, and a stubborn people. "Hear this, priests!" Hosea shouted. "Give heed, O house of Israel! Listen, O house of the king! For the judgment pertains to you. . . . Israel is defiled" (5:1, 3). Always remembering the good life God had given Israel, the prophets could get pretty fiery about sin and injustice.

It would be good for us to spend more time chewing on Leviticus, praying through the psalms, remembering the stories
of Israel's kings, and listening to the prophets. Our churches
don't do enough of that. But I hope this race through the Old
Testament gives a little taste of how scripture comes alive
when we read it as the story of God forming a people. If God
is unfolding a plan to save the whole world through Israel, it
makes sense that the Bible is full of laws and history and songs
and prophets. That's the stuff that a people needs. In the Old
Testament we get it all direct from God.

Does God Have a Plan B?

I guess the big question when we get to the New Testament
is whether God has a plan B. It seems pretty clear that the
Old Testament is about a peculiar people learning to do life
together with God and be a witness to other nations of what
the life we were made for looks like. God's Plan A looks like
saving the world through a people. But maybe Jesus came to
introduce God's Plan B. Maybe God decided that the whole
people-making project was so fraught with frustration that he
might do better to just work with one person at a time. You
know: each one reach one. Maybe God's Plan B is to save the
world through personal relationships with individuals.

Without necessarily saying it, much of the church in the West
assumes this Plan B. We read the New Testament as if it is a
spiritual self-help book, written to help me improve my relationship with God. A lot of good spiritual writing recently has
been about how the Bible isn't a list of abstract ideas that we're
supposed to learn and believe but that it's essentially relational.
(Not too long ago, I read Donald Miller's book *Searching for
God Knows What*. He makes this point quite beautifully.) It's
true that the Bible is relational—true in a way that is beautiful
and compelling. Most of us are starved for that kind of beautiful truth. But the kind of relationship scripture describes is
between God and a peculiar people. When we look closely, the

authors of the New Testament seem to go to great lengths to say that God doesn't have a Plan B.

Take Matthew, for example. The first Gospel starts with a genealogy that's full of names so hard to pronounce that we usually just skip over them. But the genealogy is hard to miss. It takes up most of the first chapter of Matthew's Gospel. At the end, Matthew says, "So all the generations from Abraham to David are fourteen generations; and from David to the deportation to Babylon, fourteen generations; and from the deportation to Babylon to the Messiah, fourteen generations" (1:17). Fourteen, fourteen, fourteen, just like that. Whoever planned this out had an eye for symmetry, and it looks to Matthew like everything is working out according to schedule. Jesus isn't an interruption to God's Plan A. He's the star of the next act in this drama.

Matthew quotes a lot of Old Testament prophecy to try to show that Jesus is the Messiah that Israel has been waiting for. But more than that, Matthew tells Jesus's story as Israel's story. Just as Israel went down to Egypt and had to come up again, Mary and Joseph take Jesus to Egypt to save him from Herod's wrath and bring him back again into the Promised Land. Just as Israel wandered for forty years in the desert, Jesus spends forty days in the desert after he is baptized by John. And just as the people of God were organized into twelve tribes, Jesus inaugurates his kingdom movement by recruiting twelve disciples to lead a new people. All of this happens in the first four chapters of Matthew.

Then, reminding his readers how Moses went up on a mountain to receive the law for God's people, Matthew says Jesus went up on a mountainside and started teaching. He blessed the assembled crowd and said to them, "Ya'll are the salt of the earth. . . . Ya'll are the light of the world" (5:13–14, according to my Okie Greek professor). Jesus didn't say that anyone who believed could take his candle and go light the world. He wasn't talking to individuals in the crowd. Jesus was talking to the crowd as a people. "A city built on a hill cannot be hid," he observed, no doubt gesturing to the crowd with a smile (5:14). There was no hiding this assembly on the hillside. The prophets had said that people would flock to God's holy mountain and worship the Lord together there, living according to God's law. When Matthew sets the scene for the Sermon on the Mount at the end of chapter 4, he is careful to note that "great crowds . . . from Galilee, the Decapolis, Jerusalem, Judea and from beyond the Jordan" gathered to listen to Jesus on the mountainside (4:25). They came from all over—from within Israel and from beyond its borders. "Do not think that I have come to abolish the Law or the Prophets," Jesus says to them. "I have come not to abolish but to fulfill" (5:17). Jesus says he is going to fulfill God's plan by gathering a people who can be a light to all the nations.

Anyone who has read the Gospels is liable to ask whether Jesus did any better at carrying out this plan than God in the Old Testament. After all, by the end of the story all the disciples are scattered and Jesus gets killed. The crowd that was gathered on that mountainside is nowhere to be found. In the crucifixion of Jesus, it looks as if God's plan fails more miserably than ever.

That is, until Jesus gets up from the dead. Here the story takes an unanticipated turn. Just when it looks like the story's greatest hope is a flop, the power of God proves stronger than the one thing that everyone thought was certain: death. (Of course we have the proverb that says two things in life are for sure: death and taxes. But Jesus also paid his taxes with money from a fish's mouth. God messes with all our certainties.) The community that forms in the book of Acts is a resurrection community—a gathering of people who believe that God raised Jesus from the dead and know that same power to be at work in their life together through the Holy Spirit. Indeed, the presence of this people is so striking that the citizens of Antioch have to create a new word to describe them. "It was in Antioch that the disciples were first called 'Christians'" (Acts 11:26).

The book of Ephesians looks back at how God made this community called church possible through Jesus. "In Christ we have . . . obtained an inheritance," it says, "having been destined according to the purpose of him who accomplishes all things according to his counsel and will" (1:11). Ephesians is as confident as Matthew that God has been unfolding a plan to save the world through a people. Jesus doesn't introduce a Plan B. Far from it. In Jesus, Ephesians says, the people called church fulfills God's Plan A. We are, by adoption, part of God's peculiar people.

When I talk to people in our neighborhood about the Rutba House and Christian community, I never use the language of "new monasticism." It just doesn't make sense to folks in Walltown. Monks, in their minds, are men in funny robes who don't talk. It doesn't help to talk about community in terms of monasticism. But the Ephesians image of adoption into God's family makes a lot of sense to people. When neighbors ask me why I live with a bunch of strange people, I tell them it's because God has adopted us into his family. These people aren't strangers to me. They're my brothers and sisters. In Christ, we're family. Now I'll admit—old and young, married and single, black, white, and brown, we're an odd-looking family. But the Bible says God wants a peculiar people, so I figure we're all right. We've been adopted by the Maker of heaven and earth.

What We Need to Play the Bible's Game

Whenever I talk with Christians about how I've learned to reread the Bible in community as God's plan to save the world through a people, someone will ask, "So are you saying that all Christians need to live in community?" I always like to start by saying, "Well, I certainly don't think we all need to live in the same house. That'd have to be a pretty big house!" Life in a new monastic community has taught me a lot about what it means to be God's people in the world, but that doesn't mean everyone needs to leave their home and family to become new monastics. God isn't calling us all to live in the same house. But I do believe God calls us through Scripture to become part of a peculiar people. If the gospel is good news for everyone, we've got to find ways to make that real for the whole church.

Or, to say it differently, every church needs to figure out how to help its people play the Bible's game. If scripture isn't meant to help us play Make Myself or Make Yourself but instead is about the game called God Makes a People, how can our churches help everyone learn to play the game we were made for? The rest of this book is an attempt to answer that question. Each of the chapters that follow is about a practice that has emerged from life together in new monastic community that could be adopted by congregations as a way of living into the story of the people of God. The stories that I tell about what these practices look like in communities are not meant as prescriptions for churches but as catalysts for imagination. My point is not that churches ought to imitate new monastic communities but that another way is possible. Too often churches feel stuck between two options, neither of which seems faithful. But in the church we're always finding our way in prayer and conversation with the people God has given us. I write with love to say, Press on! God can make a way out of no way.

Since the practices of relocation, economic redistribution, active nonviolence, grassroots ecumenism, tending a culture of grace, and submitting to the church all find their context in the story of the people of God, I want to close this chapter with a few suggestions about how churches can be intentional about playing the Bible's game. Teaching in our local church and talking to pastors and friends in other churches, I've been convinced that you can learn what a church really believes by asking what it teaches its children. This is why God said to Israel, "Keep these words that I am commanding you today in your heart. Recite them to your children and talk about them when you are at home and when you are away, when you lie down and when you rise" (Deut. 6:6–7). Deuteronomy says that the way we really believe a story as a people is by talking about it at home and on our way to other places, when we get up and when we go to bed. If that is true, then I think it's fair to say that the TV tells us our story more than the Bible. With a TV in the living room, the bedroom, and increasingly in the car, kids hear the stories that advertisers sell them when they sit at home and when they're on the road, when they lie down and when they get up. Of course we often acknowledge that this can be bad for children, and parents limit TV time. But if Deuteronomy is right, this is bad for all of us. God's law is not on our hearts when we're not impressing it on our children. (Incidentally, I think this is true whether you have biological kids or not; if we're a people, they're all our kids.) It seems that we don't tell the story of God's faithfulness enough to convince ourselves or our children that it's true. In the midst of our day-to-day lives, the story the TV tells just seems more interesting.

I'm greatly encouraged by a movement in Christian education called Godly Play.[1] In the early 1970s Jerome Berrymore, an Episcopal priest who studied the Montessori educational philosophy, developed a simple way of telling biblical stories with plain wooden figures and asking "I wonder . . ." questions that invite children into the story. This method contradicts everything people say about how kids in modern America have to have fast-paced, multimedia presentations to keep their attention. But I've heard from numerous people that it works. Not only are kids interested, but they get into the story. And for the adults doing the telling, the story gets into them. Godly Play won't work in every context (I'm thinking wooden figures on the dashboard of a car might distract the driver), but it's a good example of the sort of thing churches will have to imagine if we're going to make the story of the people of God our own.

Another movement in the American church that I find encouraging is the small group movement. These groups go by a number of names: cell groups, sharing groups, shepherding groups, family groups. What members actually do together varies more than their names. Some read the Bible, some share meals; others gather for prayer, accountability, or planning a ministry activity. But the basic idea of all these groups is this:

1. See www.godlyplay.com.

if the church is actually going to be family together, members
have to know one another. And that takes more than worshiping together on Sunday mornings.

The second thing churches need to play the Bible's game is
space for people to really know one another. One way or another, this will look like smaller groups that spend significant
time together. The people of God cannot simply be a gathering
of nuclear families, because our faith is not inherited and each
of us needs a broader support network to help us on toward
faithfulness. Neither should these smaller groups be affinity
groups where people who share common interests get together
to talk about their golf game or their hair products. The people
of God is made up of tribes where we know others who are
different from us and know ourselves more fully as we are
known and loved by the group. Whether you live with those
people or not, that is where community happens. Churches
that create such spaces for their members are like deep wells
of living water for parched and lonely souls.

We cannot overlook the fact that America's loneliness stems
from an economy that demands our allegiance when it comes to
where we live. We often acknowledge, sometimes with a hint of
pride, that ours is a mobile society. Middle-class people in our
culture feel free to relocate almost anywhere for a good education or a better job. But we ultimately do not experience this
as freedom. Without people who know us well, we feel alone.
At most we hope to spend our adult life with the person we
marry, but even marriage doesn't seem to last very well without
the context of community. Divorce is no longer a tragedy but
rather an expected heartache for the lonely traveler.

In such a culture of divorce, small groups and storytelling
will not be enough to root us in the reality of the people of God.
Churches will also have to call people into higher-commitment
membership. We have to find ways to get people to stick around.
Maybe the only way to do that is to ask people to pledge their
allegiance to the church. Of course, the minute you start talking
about allegiance to a particular community, people in America
worry that you're becoming a cult. Allegiance to the nation is

normal. Allegiance to one's family is understandable. But allegiance to a church? That makes people nervous.

But if pledging our allegiance is a way of saying who we are and where we're going, then Christians have to pledge ourselves to the people of God. If our home is in God's kingdom, we cannot pledge our ultimate allegiance to America. If God is our Father, the nuclear family cannot be our god. Instead, we've got to say that our primary commitment is to the church. But for those words to have any real meaning, churches will have to get serious about membership. We need to name our commitments to each other and develop a process to determine whether God is calling an individual to leave our community or whether the forces of the economy are simply tearing us apart. If God's plan is to save the world through a holy people, it makes sense that the devil would want to separate us. But we cannot be deceived by the devil's schemes. We should know better. After all, all those you's in our Bible are ya'lls.

5

RELOCATION AND RENEWAL

When Leah and I came back to the United States from Iraq in the spring of 2003, the most unsettling thing I did was watch the news on television. In the terminal at JFK airport, I watched images on CNN of Saddam's palaces bursting into flame and F-16s executing "surgical strikes" on military targets. Just two days before I had tried to sleep in a bed across the Euphrates River from those palaces. I had not seen on TV what it looked like for the cross-hairs of a pilot's scope to line up on a palace just before the building turned to dust. Instead, I had felt the earth shake beneath me. I had tasted the dust of death and listened to the cries of mothers who lost their children. I had seen the military targets, often hit precisely. But I had also met the man who was sleeping across the street when the bomb hit, blowing the windows out of the hotel he owned. Baghdad looked different on TV from the way it had on the ground.

The first time I saw those images on CNN, I was mad. They made it look as if bombing a city from the air didn't affect the people in it—as if buildings could be destroyed and an "oppressive regime" overturned without disturbing a modern city full

of people. I set out to tell my fellow Americans the truth. Even
though Leah and I were exhausted, we talked to every media
outlet that would listen, inviting news cameras into the living
room of our little apartment. I talked on the phone to a woman
at CNN and tried to communicate to her what we had experienced in Iraq. But she could not imagine what I was saying.
"That's just not what we're hearing and seeing," she said.

Eventually, I realized that woman was telling the truth. She
wasn't hearing and seeing the same thing I had heard and seen.
The issue wasn't that what I had seen in Iraq was true and the
images that were running on CNN were false. The difference
was that CNN staff couldn't see what I had seen. As a matter
of fact, they couldn't even imagine it. The difference in our
perspectives had everything to do with location.

We don't often think about how where we are affects what
we see and what we can imagine. Most of the time it seems
like what you see is what you get. Sure, people have different
perspectives. The tired cliché reminds us that an elephant may
feel like a hose if you're holding its trunk, like a tree if you're
touching its leg, or like a rubber mat if you feel its ear. But the
elephant is still an elephant. If all the men in the story weren't
blind, they could see that. And the point of the story is that *we
can see it*. We are not limited by our narrow perspectives. We
can see from above, almost as if from the cockpit of an F-16.
Sure, people have different perspectives. But an elephant is
an elephant, just like a war is a war. We can't even imagine
anything different.

Iraq taught me that where we locate ourselves doesn't only
change our perspective. It can also change the thing we see
and our capacity to reimagine it. We heard and saw a different
story in Iraq because we walked the streets unarmed, willing
to trust the women and men who were suffering political tur-
moil. The "embedded media" weren't lying when they showed
a different Iraq. The TV just showed what the world looks like
from behind a gun.

Not knowing if their families had survived the last night
or if they themselves would survive the next, Iraqis confessed

frustration with their own government, confusion and anger with ours. "If this is democracy, we don't want it," one man said. It was a terrible time. But it was also a time to reimagine. In bomb shelters, emergency rooms, and broken houses, we dared to imagine another way. "Please ask Mr. Bush what he would want if his family was living in Baghdad," another man said. The problem, it seemed, was that neither George Bush nor most anyone else in America could imagine the future from this location.

What I learned about location in Iraq is what the monastic tradition has known for hundreds of years: sometimes you have to relocate in order to really see the world and reimagine your role within it. That's why Antony went to the desert and Francis took to the streets. They knew something was wrong with the church, but they couldn't see any alternatives from where they were. Their location blinded them, holding their imagination captive. The monastics needed to see the world from a different place if they were going to see it anew. So they moved. And when they did, they started movements. The renewal of the church depended on relocation.

Israel's Desert Vision

God knows that relocation matters. When Moses was living in the palace in Egypt, he couldn't imagine a new life for God's people. He knew something was wrong; he even killed an Egyptian in his anger at the injustice against his people. But Moses couldn't imagine another way of life while he was living in Pharaoh's palace. So God called him out into the desert and spoke to him from a burning bush. God told Moses to bring Israel out into the desert. There the people would learn how to live—with God in the desert.

Walt Whitman wrote about how he "dreamed . . . of a city invincible,"[1] expressing a desire that's deep in most of us. People

---

1. Walt Whitman, "I Dream'd in a Dream," *Leaves of Grass*, available at Archive of Classic Poems: www.everypoet.com/Archive/Poetry/Walt_Whitman/walt_whitman_leaves_of_grass_book_05.htm.

gravitate toward the security of cities. Even when life there is a mess, we'll choose to live in a city before trying to survive on our own in the wilderness. But the God of the Bible chooses to live in a no-man's-land. Psalm 68 talks about the "mount that God desired for his abode, where the LORD will reside forever" (v. 16). We may be tempted to think God moved into the temple in Jerusalem because he had always wanted to live in the Big House, but that's not what the Bible says. God dwelled among his people in the temple, for sure. But Psalm 68 says God will live forever in the place that no one owns, on the mountain outside the city. God's home is in the abandoned place.

Why does God call the people of Israel out into the desert to receive the law and learn a new way of life? If God was willing to go live among his people in Jerusalem later, why did he make them come out into the desert first? I think it's because God wanted Israel to learn to see something that they could not see from Egypt. They had been blinded and held captive by Pharaoh's domination system. Even though they didn't like it, they were stuck in it. Or, you might say, Egypt was stuck in them. So God called the children of Israel out into the desert to help get Egypt out of their system.

But God also wanted his people to imagine a life that was inconceivable in Egypt. I think that's another reason that God called Israel out into the desert. It wasn't just that God wanted to get them out of Egypt so he could get Egypt out of them. God also wanted his people to learn to see the world from where he lives. The law of God is not a new constitution that was written after a revolution against an oppressive form of government. It is, instead, a gift from outside of human society—the careful plan of a Creator who dwells in the wild spaces of a good creation. In a forgotten place that doesn't matter to real-estate agents or city planners, the Maker of heaven and earth offers a vision for a new future—one that no one could have imagined before. It's not a vision without cities—as a matter of fact, it culminates in a city where God will live with his people. But it is, fundamentally, a desert vision. God calls Israel into the wilderness to learn to imagine a new future.

Though the great city of Jerusalem would become the City of God in Israel's imagination, God stuck with the desert vision. The biblical prophets did not measure the life of Jerusalem by comparing it with other cities of the ancient world. Instead, they held up God's desert vision as the standard. "Run to and fro through the streets of Jerusalem," God says to Jeremiah, "look around and take note! Search its squares and see if you can find one person who acts justly and seeks truth—so that I may pardon Jerusalem" (Jer. 5:1). But Jeremiah cannot find anyone who is faithful to the law of his God. So he ends up saying to God's people, "Flee for safety. . . . from the midst of Jerusalem!" (6:1). Get out of the city. Because relocation is the only hope.

In Jeremiah's day there were some prophets who said God's people should stay in Jerusalem and defend the holy city. But Jeremiah spoke against them. He said God was sending the Babylonians to sack Jerusalem as a judgment for Israel's disobedience. Jeremiah said God's people had forgotten the desert vision. They needed to go into exile, to live as aliens and strangers in a land that didn't belong to them so they could remember who God had called them to be. "For surely I know the plans I have for you," God said to the exiles through Jeremiah, "plans for your welfare and not for harm, to give you a future with hope. Then when you call upon me and come and pray to me, I will hear you" (Jer. 29:11–12). God knew that it would take relocation to win the people over again. The judgment of exile would become a gift when the people called out to God in prayer.

The book of Daniel records a prayer from Israel's exile: "Ah, LORD, great and awesome God, keeping covenant and steadfast love with those who love you and keep your commandments. . . . To the LORD our God belongs mercy and forgiveness, for we have rebelled against him" (Dan. 9:4, 9). When your home has been destroyed, your people displaced, and your life threatened, that's a pretty amazing prayer to pray to your God. Most people in the ancient world assumed that their god was dead if they were defeated in battle. They would submit to the authority of the victor's god and offer sacrifices to that god. But Daniel refused to do this. Daniel remembered the covenant God had made with Israel when he gave them the desert vision. And he repented of his people's sin. Daniel saw that God was still merciful. Indeed, the exile *was* God's mercy. Instead of letting his people destroy themselves in sin, God had relocated them. In a land that they did not own and where they were not in control, God's people remembered the desert vision and imagined new ways of living it out in all the world.

After their return from exile, God's people were never the same again. No longer concentrated around the temple in Jerusalem, their life with God found new form in synagogues scattered throughout the Greek empire. On the margins of cities that did not belong to them, God's people gathered to remember their story and anticipate the coming Messiah. A few centuries later, when the apostle Paul traveled throughout the known world to preach the good news of Jesus, he found a synagogue in most every town. Though not every synagogue welcomed him, it is clear that the church could not have spread as it did without the network of God's people scattered throughout the Roman Empire. Because they had been relocated, a new future was possible.

Opening Our Eyes and Learning to Imagine

When we gathered representatives from more than twenty communities in the summer of 2004 to name the characteristic marks of new monastic communities, "relocation to the abandoned places of Empire" was the first mark we named.[2] As we told our stories to one another, we heard how God had called many of us out of places of power—Washington, DC, corporate America, suburban megachurches, top-flight universities. The patterns of life we had learned in those places had seemed to hold us captive, making it hard to even imagine

2. Rutba House, ed., *School(s) for Conversion: Twelve Marks of a New Monasticism* (Eugene, OR: Wipf and Stock, 2005), 10–25.

other possibilities. We knew that it was hard to be a Christian, but we didn't know any other way. Often unsure of the road ahead, almost all of us had left some part of our life behind. People had quit their job, dropped out of school, moved their family across country, and given up former ambitions—all for the sake of a new life in places no one had heard of before (unless they read the crime logs). Waterfront South. Silk Hope. Walltown. The Badlands. What good would you look for in the Badlands?

From her community in the Badlands, Sister Margaret McKenna writes, "My journey . . . has had one consistent direction: away from the distortions in my heart caused by the spirit of Empire, and towards God and the New Jerusalem, the Beloved Community of Her dreams and ours."[3] Sr. Margaret's community, New Jerusalem, has been in one of Philadelphia's worst neighborhoods for fifteen years. But there she has found hope, making God's dreams her own. I'll admit, Sr. Margaret's kind of relocation seems counterintuitive. It isn't a story of climbing the ladder. Neither is it your typical "simpler is better" story (believe me, there's nothing simple about living with fifty addicts in recovery). Sr. Margaret and other new monastics have relocated to abandoned inner-city neighborhoods and neglected farms because they believe that God is teaching them to see there. In the abandoned places we learn to get Egypt out of our system.

The Camden House community in the Waterfront South neighborhood of Camden, New Jersey, has learned what environmental racism means by relocating to one of the poorest neighborhoods in America. (Incidentally, Camden was once among America's most promising cities. Walt Whitman's poem "I Dream'd a Dream," which I quoted earlier, was inspired by his time in Camden.) Fresh out of college in 2003, most of the community members moved into Camden in the hot and humid summer, when the stench from the local sewage treatment plant is often so strong it makes kids in the neighborhood

3. Ibid., 25.

park vomit. What they learned after doing some research was that sewage from multiple cities and suburbs in New Jersey was all getting pumped into their neighborhood for treatment. Upper-middle-class neighborhoods had organized "Not in My Backyard" campaigns to prevent the construction of treatment plants in their communities. And they had been successful. So the sewage from all those communities followed the path of least resistance to Waterfront South.

Where I grew up in rural North Carolina, we had a saying for folks who seemed pretentious. It wasn't the nicest thing to say about someone, but it made the point. We'd say, "He don't think his sh-t stinks." Now, maybe all of us are tempted sometime to think that we're better than others. But whoever gets the sewage plant in their backyard knows too well that everyone's sewage stinks the same. People in Cherry Hill, New Jersey (a posh suburb of Camden with good schools), may never think of the kids down in Waterfront South, Camden. But the kids who attend Sacred Heart School, just across the street from Camden House, can't forget the smell of their neighbors in communities miles and miles away.

It may be hard to teach the concept of environmental racism to students, even at a college level. But everyone at Camden House gets it. Relocation has, in a sense, taken their blinders off. When they think about public policy now, they think about how it affects neighborhoods with the least ability to stand up for themselves. When they hear someone say, "Not in my backyard!" they ask, "Then in whose?" They can't help but ask. After all, the answer affects them and people they love dearly.

A couple of years ago I got arrested in Raleigh, our state capital, for trying to prevent an execution at Central Prison. It wasn't the first time. The magistrate got mad and set a five-thousand-dollar bail, so I was stuck in jail until I could go before a judge. I don't know that I would have chosen it, but jail was an incredible education. The receiving unit was so overcrowded that I wasn't assigned a cell. Instead, an officer gave me a mat to lie on and said I could put it down anywhere in the common area. It was hard to find a place on the floor that someone else hadn't already claimed, but when I did sit down I struck up a conversation with the guy next to me. He asked what I was doing there. I told him how I had tried nonviolently to stop an execution. His response caught me off guard: "The train starts here, you know."

"What train?" I asked.

"The train that goes to Death Row. Man, look around this room. All these brothers are from the same neighborhoods. They know each other before they get here. But they get caught for something and brought in. And the train starts here. It starts here, and it ends over there at Death Row."

This fellow wanted to help me learn to see. I thought about the young guys I know in Walltown—kids who come to Leah's after-school program and my Bible class on Wednesday nights. I thought about how some of them might end up on that train because they were from the wrong neighborhood, and I knew that it was wrong. I knew we had to work to stop the train. God made those kids in Walltown just the same as every other child on this earth. And God doesn't love them any less because their families are broken or poor or hooked on crack. Maybe Christians anywhere can see the truth of that. But I didn't know in my gut that I had to do something about it until I relocated to Walltown, spent a night in jail, and got an education from the fellow on the mat next to mine.

So relocation has opened our eyes to issues we need to address in our homes and our communities. It has helped us see some of the Egypt that was in our system without us even knowing it. But relocation is also teaching new monastic communities to reimagine how we address issues of poverty, racism, and capital punishment (among lots and lots of others). Sarah Jobe at Rutba House says that she realized not too long ago that she has given up on "Master Plans." She realized this when someone asked her what the goal of the Rutba House is. Sarah says she used to think you identify problems and then you fix them by whatever means seems most effective. That's how she had been taught to think. But after relocating to Walltown, she started to see that problems aren't that simple. Often the "fixers" are part of the problem without even knowing it themselves. And sometimes the way people with power go about fixing problems just makes things worse. Sarah says she has learned in Walltown that what's wrong with the world is much bigger than our ability to fix it, no matter how good our plan. So she has given up on Master Plans. And she is learning to pray.

New monastics who relocate to the places that society has abandoned are not heroes. Maybe some of us wanted to be heroes when we got into this, but we are learning that heroes are not what God needs. And they're not what our communities need either. What we need, more than anything, are people who will relearn God's desert vision in the places we do not own, where we are not in control. What we need is people who will learn to cry out to God as Daniel did, repenting of the ways we've sinned against God and remembering the great mercy of the way of life God has given. We do not need power to live in the Way of Jesus. Indeed, power often distracts us. But in the places that people in power think unimportant, we are free to experiment in the truth of God's law. We are free to imagine what God's kingdom could look like, right here on earth as it is in heaven. I don't pretend that we're getting everything right in new monastic communities—no more than Israel got everything right in the wilderness. But we're in a space where we are free to imagine. And that means a new future is possible. In some cases, it may already be here.

Imagining Church from the Margins

I said at the end of the last chapter that I don't think every Christian is called to live in a new monastic community. Just for the record, I don't think every Christian in Durham needs to move to Walltown. (Walltown would hardly be an "abandoned place" if that happened.) But I do want to ask what the church in every city can learn from new monastic experiments with relocation. What could it mean to reimagine church from the margins of our cities and towns? How might

God's desert vision inform our mission and life together in congregations?

More than anything else, relocation is teaching us that God is at work in the people and places that society has given up on. It's hard for churches to confess that we have given up on people, but I think we start to see it when we take an honest look at who we are reaching out to. This is what church-growth consultants call our "target audience." It's the group of people whom we invite to become our brothers and sisters in the family of God. People have argued about whether it is better for churches to have a narrow or broad target audience, but that is not my concern here. My worry, instead, is that the audience we assume usually keeps us from knowing people who aren't like us and learning the things we most need to know.

On the one hand, some of our churches practice what I like to call "spiritual Reaganomics." These churches (or parachurch organizations) believe that when you reach the people who have the greatest influence in society with the good news of Jesus, the message will trickle down through their spheres of influence. In this case, the target audience is popular kids in high schools or powerful players in Washington, DC. The strategy is to go after them, hoping that once they're on God's team they'll use their influence and power to spread the gospel far and wide.

On the other hand, some churches and Christian organizations practice mission as a means of compassion and liberation. These Christians target the poor and offer them relief services. Or they target the oppressed and promise to fight for their human rights. These groups may opt for direct political engagement, or they may simply do relief and development without questioning the status quo. But in either case, the idea here is not to use another's power to spread a spiritual message but rather to use your own social power to uplift and empower others.

Unfortunately, neither of these models necessarily recognizes the presence of God in and among those people whom society overlooks. On the one side the church has a message that we hope will trickle down to the masses, while on the other we offer relief and development to others and their problems. But rarely do we acknowledge how little we trust Jesus when he says, "Blessed are the poor . . . blessed are those who mourn . . . blessed are the meek . . . blessed are those who hunger and thirst for righteousness" (Matt. 5:3–6). We make little effort to really know the people Jesus blessed. Even less do we try to learn from them how to inherit the kingdom of heaven.

What we're learning in new monastic communities is that the renewal of the church depends on our relocating. So if God is moving your congregation to relocate to an overlooked or abandoned neighborhood, I don't want to get in the way of that. But neither do I think that's the only way forward. One of the things I want to suggest is that churches might experiment with relocating Christian education. Acknowledging our need to learn from people who are overlooked and forgotten, we could leave our Sunday school rooms and go study with those people on their turf. Maybe the youth Bible study at your church could move to the group home in town and read Jesus's parables together with troubled teens. Or maybe the adult men's Sunday school class could study its lesson together with men in a local prison. If your church has a peace and justice study group, why not try to learn from those who hunger and thirst for justice because their lives depend on it? I know churches often go to nursing homes or prisons or soup kitchens to "do ministry." And some real good comes from that. But that's not what I'm suggesting. What if we went to the abandoned places to learn with and from the people there?

I have a friend in Durham named Ann Atwater. During the civil rights movement, Ann was one of the most militant black leaders in town. She likes to say, "I hollered till they listened." (And sometimes she'll wink and whisper, "If they didn't, I'd burn their house down.") But Ann's whole life changed when she was asked to cochair a ten-day meeting to plan the integration of Durham public schools. The person who was asked to cochair the committee with Ann was C. P. Ellis, the local leader of the Ku Klux Klan. Neither of them wanted to work with the other, but a shrewd federal organizer convinced them that if they didn't lead, the usual power-brokers of the black and white communities would step in. So Ann and C. P. accepted the invitation, and in the course of ten days together their lives were changed. In a series of events that can only be described as miraculous, Ann and C. P. realized that their kids were suffering the same things and joined together to work for a better Durham. More than that, they became friends. On the last night of the meetings they chaired, C. P. Ellis stood in front of the crowd and tore up his Klan card.[4]

Ann is in her seventies now and has a wealth of wisdom. On top of that, she's a teacher at heart. So I asked her about a year ago if she would help me with a little experiment in relocating education. We decided we'd invite members of churches around Durham to study Mark's Gospel with us at the local homeless shelter. When we got there, we invited the folks staying at the shelter to study with us. They were a little slow to join us at first, so Ann asked a few guys what it would take to get more people there. "Fried chicken," one man quipped. So Ann said, "All right! Next week I'll have fifty pieces of fried chicken." And she did. By the time we finished Mark, we had a group of about twenty people—half from the shelter, half from churches around town. Frank, a member of the local Catholic parish, reflected on his experience of our "Word on the Street" Bible study:

> Some of us *have* made a studied effort to avoid looking into the eyes of those who *have not*. We're afraid to stop and talk—afraid, I guess, that we'll be asked for money or, worse, to hear a story that might move us to act in some more meaningful way. That fear, I think, can make life for us a living hell. So I welcomed the opportunity to break down the barriers and help remind me that . . . their poverty is our poverty. We dare not let an accident of birth separate us from the suffering felt by others.

4. Ann Atwater and C. P. Ellis's story has been told in Osha Gray Davidson's book *The Best of Enemies: Race and Redemption in the New South* (New York: Scribner, 1996) and in Diane Bloom's documentary *An Unlikely Friendship* (Filmaker's Library, 2002).

Men who had every right to curse the heavens expressed instead a faith in God that was, under the circumstances, sublime. When we share the Word across the well-etched lines of race and class, we're forced to see ourselves in our most elemental form. In this context, it is our deepest afflictions and crippling addictions and highest aspirations that become our most prominent features, and God alone is our hope.

Reading scripture at the shelter, we've learned to see a bit of what Israel learned in the desert—that God alone is our hope and that we are called to be a people together, even across the dividing lines that we so often assume. That's what I long for churches in America to learn together with the homeless and the imprisoned, the forgotten and the neglected. It is the sort of renewal that we can experience only by taking relocation seriously. But in the same breath that I say that, I want to say this too: you probably won't have to go any farther than the forgotten edges of your church's membership to find people and places that have been abandoned and neglected. Our first step in relocation should always be to see how far we are from those people we are bound to in baptism.

The minute we do that, we have to start talking about gospel economics. And that's the subject of our next chapter.

6

DAILY BREAD AND FORGIVEN DEBTS

In our morning and evening prayers at Rutba House, we pray the Lord's Prayer every day. More and more, I like to pray it with my eyes open. "Thy kingdom come, thy will be done, on earth as it is in heaven," we say. Right here, with these people, we pray for God's kingdom to come. It's been a surprising experience to say those words with the same people every day, year after year. You might think the words would become redundant, like the instructions attendants give at the beginning of every airline flight on how to buckle your seatbelt and use your cushion as a flotation device. You might think a prayer that you pray twice a day every day would become words you just say while you think about something else. But when I pray for God's kingdom to come in this place as it is in heaven, I actually want it a little more each day. I know how far we are from it. But I also feel how much we need it. It's sort of like checking the map on a long road trip. Every time you look at it, you get a little more excited about getting to where you're going.

When we pray, "Give us this day our daily bread, and forgive us our debts as we forgive our debtors," I think about putting food on the table and paying the bills. Now, I'll admit those might not be the most pious thoughts. But in the context of community, they do seem to follow up pretty well on our request for God's reign to come in this place at it is in heaven. If we're going to have a life together here with God and one another, we need God to show us how to put food on the table and pay the bills. After all, if you ask most people why they live the way they do, they say they work the job they work and do the chores they do to put food on the table and pay the bills. These are pretty basic needs for all of our lives. But these needs can also become tyrants, dictating a narrow set of possibilities for how we live. We are tempted to imagine that we are bound by economic necessity. But the Bible tells us that life as it is is not the life we were made for. There is a better way. There is a kingdom not of this world—a "kingdom of heaven," Matthew's Gospel calls it. And like all kingdoms, this one has a way of putting food on the table and paying the bills. To put it briefly, God has an economy.

God's Economy Starts at Home

The minute I start taking about Christianity and the economy, someone always asks whether I'm really just a communist in disguise, trying to use Jesus to argue for a new economic order. At the same time, someone else always worries that I'm using Jesus to justify advanced capitalism, as has been done so many times before. Because when we talk about the economy, whatever our convictions, we think we know the options. It's either Karl Marx or Adam Smith—communism or capitalism. This is, of course, a spectrum, and there are options in between. But every economic system aims to answer the same question: what is the best way to organize the relationship between people and their money?

The French sociologist and lay theologian Jacques Ellul summarized our normal way of thinking about money like this: "We look at the money question from its global perspective, and we try to solve the whole economic problem in order to solve, once and for all, the problem of money."[1] But the question of which system best organizes our relationship to money doesn't seem very important to the Bible. Because the Bible is primarily concerned with our relationship to God. Sure, the Bible talks a lot about money. But it's in the context of our relationship with the God who made us and everything else that is or ever will be. In the Lord's Prayer we are not instructed to ask for the system that will best facilitate global economic relations. Instead, we ask God to provide today's food and cancel our debts, even as we are canceling debts owed us. Instead of taking the global view, you might say God begins with us at home.

The word *economy* comes from two Greek words: *oikos* (house or home) and *nomos* (law or order). So the *oikonomia* is, literally, the order of the home. There's nothing peculiarly Christian about that. It's just how people thought about society in the ancient world. You might think of it this way: if a kingdom is a huge building where all kinds of people can live, the fundamental building blocks for this huge structure are homes. Households are the base units of the economy.

In the modern world, people who have wanted to significantly change the economic order have, for the most part, organized national revolutions. Some of these have been violent, like the communist revolution in China or the establishment of democratic capitalism in Central America. Some have also been nonviolent, like the defeat of the British imperial economy in India or the fall of communism in Eastern Europe. But all these revolutions have been movements to reorganize the national economic system, because that's where we think change happens.

Any strategy to reorganize a system assumes a certain amount of control. And only those people who can imagine themselves in power set out to change the system. Democracy has taught us that people power can be just as effective as firepower. But whatever the case, power makes the

1. Jacques Ellul, *Money and Power* (Downers Grove, IL: InterVarsity Press, 1979), 11.

difference in political revolutions. If only we can get enough power, we believe that we can set the world back on the right track.

This makes God's economy seem strange. In our way of thinking, the God who is all-powerful should be able to effect greater change than any government or army or grassroots movement. But God doesn't propose an economic system. The Creator doesn't come down on the side of Karl Marx or Adam Smith. Instead, he gives a peculiar set of instructions to households.

After liberating a bunch of slaves from an oppressive economic order, God teaches them a new home order. Here's how it worked: every day you went out to gather enough food for that day from the manna and quails that God provided. There was more than enough for everyone. But if you gathered more than you could eat, it would be eaten by maggots in the night. The next day you went out and God provided again. That was the new economy: each day, daily bread.[2]

Every sixth day God said you could gather enough for two days and then take a break on the seventh. So on Friday night the maggots didn't show up, and there was enough for everyone to eat their fill on Saturday. God's manna in the desert was supposed to teach Israel an economics of providence that they would continue to live out even after they had their own vines and fig trees. Every seventh year, God said they could take a sabbatical—not to do that big project they hadn't had time to do but to rest in God's provision and celebrate the abundance of this economy. And on the fiftieth year, after seven times seven years, all debts were to be forgiven, all people set free from economic bondage, and all land returned to the households God had originally given it to.

Of course, this economy was part of a whole way of life in which God's people were invited to live at peace with one

2. As I was writing at Rutba House this morning, a kind woman named Nancy brought us four garbage bags full of day-old bread from a local bakery. She said it would have gone into a dumpster otherwise. Instead, it's become our daily bread. Better to spread it around than to let the maggots eat it in the dumpster.

another and their Maker. God did not propose the manna economy as a better system for ordering economic relations for all people. The Jews never debated the Philistines as to whether God's economy was more efficient or productive than their economic system. The economy of daily bread and forgiven debts was, instead, a gift God's people could receive and invite others into. They could put it into practice right where they were. In the no-man's-land that no one owned or controlled, Israel learned to put food on the table and pay their bills by reliance on God's goodness alone.

God's Answer to Poverty Is a Broken Body

When it comes to the practice of economics, I think this is what new monastic communities have been learning: God is offering us the gift of an economy that we can start living right now, wherever we are. Spending time on the margins of society, we have seen the incredible divide between the haves and the have-nots. We know that economic injustice is at the heart of the disease that is crippling our communities. But we have opted not to put our hope in "compassionate conservatism" or a "New Society." We haven't joined the Communist Workers Party. We're not waiting for the revolution. Instead, we've tried to follow the Spirit's lead by reorganizing our households around the manna economy God has already given us.

Patrick and Mary are some friends of ours who started a Catholic Worker community nearly twenty years ago. Not long after they moved into their house, they met a Mexican woman at their parish who was on her own with three small children. She was struggling to make ends meet, so Patrick and Mary invited her and the kids to come and live with them. How could they share the Eucharist at church on Sunday morning and not share their table at home? If God had made them family, they reasoned, God could provide for their needs.

So they moved in together and shared what they had. Through a variety of jobs, donations, and food "redeemed" from dumpsters, they always had more than enough. They prayed for daily bread and kept going, trusting that God would provide. Today all three of the children who moved in with Patrick and Mary when they were homeless kids have grown up, gotten jobs, married, and moved to other places. But Patrick told me not long ago that each of them sends a check almost every month to support their house of hospitality. They believe in God's manna economy because they've seen it.

"Because there is one bread," the apostle Paul says of the Lord's Supper, "we who are many are one body, for we all partake of the one bread" (1 Cor. 10:17). I guess that's why Jesus didn't teach us to pray, "Give *me* this day *my* daily bread." We really are in this together. If the daily bread we pray for and the bread of life God gives us is about a new economy, that means it's about *our* money and how we use it in relationship to God and one another. We cannot blame the economic system we live under. We cannot wait for the revolution. We can't and we don't have to, because God has already given us a new economic order.

Just what a household's economy looks like varies from one new monastic community to another, but all of this talk about household economies becomes real only in concrete practice, so it's worth looking at a few different examples. Some communities practice what's called a strict common purse. They read Acts where it says, "No one claimed private ownership of any possessions, but everything they owned was held in common" (4:32), and they decided to put all their money into one bank account (like couples do when they get married). Out of that account, most common purse communities pay for everyone's living expenses and then use the rest to bless others or support the work of God's people. Jesus People USA in Chicago is a good example of this. Years ago they started a roofing-supply business that is now one of the largest in Chicago. Lots of folks from the community work for the company in all the different positions that it takes to make a company run. But the business manager gets the same living allowance as the guy loading shingles on the stock floor. This means that at the end of the day, the business makes a lot of money. But instead of hoarding their profits, the folks at JPUSA use income from their "mission business" to run homeless shelters on the north side of Chicago. Folks from the community work to prepare meals, get beds ready, sweep floors, and help homeless folks find permanent housing. And at the end of the day, they get the same living allowance as their fellow community members who work for the roofing-supply company.

Common purses work well for communities that share common work. Our friends at Jubilee Partners in Georgia, for example, keep a common purse and work together to run a farm and resettle hundreds of refugees each year. As they share life together on the farm, it's amazing how little the folks there can live on. But even they have experienced the effects of inflation. A couple of years ago, they decided to increase each person's living allowance from ten to fifteen dollars a week. One of Jubilee's partners, Al Lawler, says that's the only time in his life that he's ever received a 50 percent raise!

In communities where people don't share common work, a strict common purse is hard to maintain. There are just a lot more variables. Which·means you have to have a lot of conversations. I mean, a lot. The folks at Church of the Sojourners in San Francisco decided years ago that those conversations didn't necessarily lead to deeper discipleship. They wanted to celebrate God's economy together, not nitpick over the details of whether someone really needed a new pair of shoes. So they decided to agree on a standard of living. They figured out what it costs to run their households and divided that by the number of adults in the community. After people give a tithe out of their income each month, they pay that living expense to the community. Beyond that amount for food, rent, and utilities, the community has agreed on a common standard for what they call "discretionary" spending. That means the money you spend on the clothes you wear and the trips you take and the coffee you drink and the books you buy. In San Francisco (which is a pretty expensive city), they agreed to each live on $275 of discretionary money per month. Of course you don't *have* to spend that much. But the community has agreed that no one will spend more than that. Whatever money people make above their living expenses and discretionary allotment they put in an account to give away.

As I said, not all communities do economic sharing the same way. But we do share a conviction that it really is possible to share what we have in common and trust God for our daily bread. If someone loses their job, we're able to take care of them until they can find a new one. If an employer tells someone in our community they have to uproot their life and family, they have the freedom to say no. This is not to say that there aren't hard times. Some communities have made real sacrifices to take care of one another. But we can pour out our lives for each other with joy because we know Jesus has given himself for us. His broken body is our daily bread. We receive it gladly, thanking God that we have an alternative to the Wonder Bread of this world.

A Cup Running Over

The stories we hear about money are mostly stories about scarcity. The reason we have economics, I learned in college, is because of scarcity. There's just not enough stuff for everyone to get what they want. We've got limited resources and un-limited desires. So human beings develop systems to organize our economic relations and try to make sure everyone gets enough. We try to dream up the system that will best deliver the resources to the people who need them. We do this because we have to in order to survive.

Rarely do we question this basic story. As I've already said, most debates about economics simply ask which of the systems that people have dreamed up best distributes the limited re-sources available to us. We accept the assumption of scarcity. But Jesus didn't. Matthew tells a story about how Jesus taught and healed all day once in a deserted place where a crowd had followed him. About suppertime, when the disciples were no doubt starting to get hungry themselves, they came to Jesus and said, "This is a deserted place, and the hour is now late; send the crowds away so that they may go into the villages and buy food for themselves" (Matt. 14:15). The disciples were being economic realists. There wasn't enough food in that deserted place for all those people. Two fish and five loaves of bread— that was all they had. But Jesus said, "They need not go away, you give them something to eat" (14:16).

Jesus didn't buy the assumption of scarcity. He didn't buy it because he knew a different story about how the world works. In the beginning, Jesus remembered, the earth was dark and void of any resources. But God spoke and there was light. God spoke and there was land, water, trees, and fish. John says of Christ, "All things came into being through him, and without him not one thing came into being" (John 1:3). Jesus knew a story that didn't begin with scarcity but with God.

If God is who the Bible says he is, then there is an economy of abundance that is more real than the stories of scarcity that we know. Matthew says that Jesus took the two fish and five loaves, gave thanks, and broke the bread. He broke it just as he would later break the bread that he called his body. And he gave it to the disciples. "You give them something to eat," he had told them. And it had sounded like nonsense. But they did. The disciples shared what they had and, miraculously, it was more than enough. "And all ate and were filled, and they took up what was left over of the broken pieces, twelve baskets full" (14:20).

I can't explain to you how that happened on a hillside in Galilee two thousand years ago. Just as I can't explain how Jesus poured out his blood to give us life, but still had enough life in him to get up from the dead. Jesus could do it because Jesus is God. But I can't explain that to you. It does seem clear to me, however, that if we have any hope of salvation, it is because of the miracle of God's abundance. And if we believe the story of justification by faith, I guess we ought to receive the gift of God's economy by faith too. Because the Bible seems to say that they're the same thing. We pray, "Give us this day our daily bread," and Jesus says, "This is my body, broken for you." We ask

God for life, and Jesus pours out his blood, not holding back. Because Jesus doesn't believe in scarcity. The One who made the world out of nothing knows that he always has more than enough to give to his children.

Maybe the most radical thing about God's economy is that it frees us to be generous. Jesus said, "Give to everyone who begs from you" (Matt. 5:42), but I don't think we believe he really meant it. How could you possibly give to whoever asks? There are limited resources and unlimited requests. Wouldn't you go broke? Not if the Jesus who calls us to generosity is the One who created everything out of nothing and fed five thousand with two fishes and five loaves of bread. One of the things I've learned in community is that as we receive the gift of God's economy, we are able to better practice the generosity that Jesus thought possible.

As I've already mentioned, common purses not only make it possible for communities to take care of one another but also free up money to be shared generously with friends and neighbors and those in need. At Rutba House each month we set aside money that we're able to share with people we know in the neighborhood. If someone asks for a loan, we can usually give it to them. If a friend gets stuck, we try to help them out.

Some of us have worked for social service agencies, but we don't want to be an agency or to give our money to charities that will manage the poor for us. Most poor people know that agencies are part of the economic system that assumes scarcity. Many of them participate in that system, doing whatever they can to get enough for themselves. Often that means lying to a social worker, stealing, begging, or forfeiting their own dignity in some other way. But if that same person is my neighbor, we can share what we have, celebrating God's provision and affirming one another as children of God. We can give loans and pay each other back. Or a friend who needs money can loan me something in return. I borrowed a leaf blower last week from a friend down the street to whom we gave a car a couple of years ago. She has also hosted friends of ours on her couch when we had more guests than we could fit in our houses. According to the IRS, we're both poor. But in our relationship of sharing, we feel rich.

Now I'm not saying that generosity always overcomes the deep divisions that exist between the haves and the have-nots. We have invited people to live with us only to watch them steal from us. We've given loans that haven't been repaid. In short, we have been used. But unlike a social service agency, we can have an honest conversation with those people when they come back again, if they ever do. (Over the years, folks come back around more often than you might think.) Because we have a relationship, we can talk honestly about our pain and our concern for one another. And we can try to be reconciled. I'm not saying that it always happens or that we're very good at it. But God invites us into a context where it's possible. And sometimes, by grace, the miracle of reconciliation really does happen.

Celebration as Resistance

Dorothy Day of the Catholic Worker movement used to say, "Our problems stem from our acceptance of this filthy rotten system." We are too much at home in a world where thousands of children die each day from hunger while some parents spend thousands of dollars to get their kids to lose weight. Our relationships and communities are broken by a filthy rotten system. Most of us just accept that this is the way things are. We could wish it otherwise, but we know we don't have the power to change the system, so we accept it and go on. A few courageous souls in almost every generation defy realism, rise up, and try to change the system. Some even give their lives resisting economic exploitation and systems of death. But the revolutionaries who survive inevitably find themselves unable to live into the future they imagined. Often they end up perpetuating the same injustices they protested in their youth.

Whether we accept or rebel against the filthy rotten system, it feels like we are enslaved by its power. The "global economy" seems to have an infinite ability to draw people into its orbit—even those who struggle hardest to resist it. So protesters boost the oil economy by flying to DC by the thousands to tell the president they don't want a war for oil. In the face of Empire, it is easy to grow cynical and give up. The cynic can criticize every TV commercial and World Bank decision as well as every attempt to resist the system, but he or she ultimately accepts the "filthy rotten system" by going on as if it is the only economy that's possible in this world.

But the Empire's economy isn't the only possibility. God's economy insists on interrupting the filthy rotten system. And it does it with a celebration—what the Old Testament calls a feast. Because people are twisted by sin, God knew that injustice would creep into Israel and cause economic divisions between brothers and sisters. But God was determined to interrupt this slouch toward a filthy rotten system with redistribution parties. I already mentioned the big feast of Israel—the Year of Jubilee that God commanded the people to celebrate every fifty years. But there were lots of feasts in Israel where the people were called together to celebrate God's goodness and share the bounty of harvest. Each celebration was an act of resistance against the power of Mammon.

New monastic communities have learned not to underestimate the power of celebrating the gifts God has already given us. Just this past weekend I was with the good folks at Communality. It's a church community of about thirty people, living in multiple households in downtown Lexington, Kentucky. Like most Southern towns, Lexington has a history of racial division. "Bad" neighborhoods are poor and black, while "good" neighborhoods are white and middle class. One of Communality's households is in a poor and black neighborhood. The community has made it a practice to throw regular parties at that house. Everyone from the community comes together to fellowship and share food. But they also invite all their neighbors to come and join the feast. When I was there, black and white neighbors with very different economic backgrounds shared a potluck meal together. People brought what they had, we blessed it, and everyone ate their fill. Unlike a soup kitchen or a breadline, however, the well-off didn't serve the less privileged. We all ate together. And as we ate, we talked about our lives and the neighborhood and what folks thought needed to happen. In the course of conversation, I learned that this neighborhood that eats together regularly mobilized a couple of years ago to resist an urban revitalization plan that would have displaced the poor from their homes. Their meals became more than meals, by God's grace. They became the sorts of celebrations that make resistance possible.

Because the people of God are called together to bless all the peoples of the earth, we can't step back from public engagement with the filthy rotten system that crushes many of God's children. But neither do we resist it with the weapons of the world. New monasticism has been learning that celebration is our best tactic of resistance. We celebrate because God has already given to us the daily bread and debt forgiveness that we need to end poverty now. But we also rejoice that we have good news to share with representatives of this world's governments and corporate power players. Everyone is invited to God's party. Rich and poor alike can come and join the feast. Every other economy is ultimately going to be destroyed, we know. But there's good news! We have the chance to invite everyone we meet into something that will last. Our resistance does not come from fear that we will destroy ourselves if we do not take care of the poor, even though that is true. It does not even come from anger, though there are good reasons to be angry with the filthy rotten system. Instead, we resist out of joy, like lovers who fight off sleep to enjoy one another. We defy the filthy rotten system when we share our bread with neighbors and remember the manna economy God has given us to enjoy.

The Generosity-Driven Church

A few years ago some people from new monastic communities got together with other Christians around the country and started something called the Relational Tithe. Darin Petersen really caught a vision for the difference generosity can make when it's tied to relationships. Since Darin is an organizer, he started figuring out how people in the church could share a tithe of their income with the widows and the poor—the economically vulnerable for whom the Bible calls us to care. Using the Internet, Darin developed a system to organize regional clusters of people who pool money and agree together on how to share it with the people we know. In a matter of days, we're able to meet economic needs of friends and neighbors who are struggling. Darin likes to say that there's never more than one degree of separation between the giver and the receiver in the RT. Through direct relationships in our neighborhoods, we share the wealth of God's economy with those who need it most. But that also means that I get to share some of my money with friends and neighbors of people in Philadelphia, Oakland, Nigeria, and Indonesia. It has been amazing to watch how well this system works. Often the requests aren't huge, but we have consistently met every genuine need that members have brought to the group over the past few years. It's an incredible thing to know you're part of a network that will help you take care of anyone you know who is in need.

What I've learned from the Relational Tithe is that Christians really can celebrate God's economy together. Not all of us live in community. Not all of us are in the same place. But we all pray, "Give us this day our daily bread, and forgive us our debts as we forgive our debtors." Energized by a vision for how to make our prayer real in daily practice, we've come together in a network that makes real economic sharing among God's people possible. If you're interested in using the technology that the RT has developed for economic sharing in your church or community, you can visit www.relationaltithe.org to learn more.

But before you do that, let me encourage you to ask how you could make economic considerations more relational within your church. This may be the biggest obstacle we face when it comes to celebrating God's economy together. We tend to think that our finances are individual decisions that we make apart from our brothers and sisters at church. Maybe we get together to talk about the church budget. Maybe the pastor even gives a sermon about how much of our money we need to give to the church. But we don't talk much about what we do with the rest of our money. We especially don't talk about how our relationships are economic. But they are.

Think, for example, about how many members of your church have left because their job took them somewhere else. Economic decisions really do affect our relationships—and not just when they end them. If we really are God's family together in the church, one couple's decision to buy a vacation home really does affect their relationship with a single mom in the church who is working two jobs to pay rent and put food on the table. It's hard to imagine how they could have an honest relationship with each other, even when they're part of the same church.

I'm not trying to say what should happen in this case. There are a thousand things to consider, and there are no easy answers. But I do wonder what would happen if we all rethought our financial decisions in terms of the relationships we've been given in the body of Christ. What if in Christ we really are bound to every other person who has been joined to Christ's body? If our theology is true, there are a lot of people to think of any time we consider our finances.

Not the least of whom are the particular people we worship with week after week. What if every time we made a job decision, we were to ask, "How will this affect my relationships at church?" Maybe we wouldn't go for the biggest paycheck or even for the most fulfilling work. After all, if we find our meaning in being part of God's people, we don't have to find it in our work. Maybe if we thought in terms of relationships, we'd work together with brothers and sisters more often. Some friends of ours who were sent by their church to live missionally in an urban neighborhood decided to start their own housecleaning business. They didn't do it because they could make a ton of money or because they felt called to housecleaning.

They did it because they wanted to be together. Of course, being together is not the only way to prioritize relationships. Married couples often decide to have one spouse work more so that the other can take care of children or serve the community. This kind of arrangement might happen more often among folks in churches if we talked openly about how our economic decisions are relational.

But relationships alone are not enough. Because we've all had bad relationships. Family is great, but there is such a thing as a dysfunctional family. And most of us have experienced it in one way or another. Ultimately, I don't think it's enough to let relationships drive our financial decisions. We need more. We need the generosity that flows from God's abundance. Instead of basing our economic decisions on what we can do or achieve, we need to remember the gifts God has already given us. We need to become generosity-driven churches.

Some years ago, a church I know well decided to launch a building campaign. They were a healthy church with a good pastor, and new members kept coming every month. It was a rural congregation whose size was somewhat limited by the community that surrounded it. If every living soul for five miles around found Jesus, they could probably have still fit in their building. But some folks in the congregation had heard about church growth and started thinking that they needed to build a larger sanctuary along with new classrooms and "multipurpose" space. So they launched a building campaign. Through the denomination they hired a fundraising expert who organized an ambitious effort, seeking to raise millions of dollars. But after the church had been at it a number of years and reached only about half of the goal, they decided to end the campaign. Some people felt like it was a failure. They didn't have enough money to build their big new building.

But since they could still fit in the old one, they looked around and asked what else they might use the money for. It turned out that one family that had come to the church during this time of growth didn't have much money. The father was disabled, and they struggled to make ends meet. But the church was genuinely glad to have them and really enjoyed the gifts they brought to the community. So the church decided to use some of the money from the campaign fund to build that family a house.

That's what I mean when I talk about a generosity-driven church. Don't get me wrong: churches need meeting spaces, and I'm not opposed to building new ones when they're needed. But a generosity-driven church that builds houses for the poor will never have to worry about church growth. A church that pours itself out as Christ gave himself for the church will always be budding with new life.

7

A NEW PEACE CORPS

Not long after September 11, 2001, I had a conversation with Fred, my pastor at the time. I can't remember just what we were discussing, but Fred has a way of saying things right in the middle of a conversation that you remember long after you've forgotten what it is you were talking about. So I remember Fred saying in the middle of a conversation about something that I thought important at the time, "I think every generation has a defining moment—an experience that everyone shares and is significant enough that it shapes everyone's life from then on.

"For my generation, it was Vietnam," Fred said. "For you, I think it will be September 11th."

When Fred said that, I thought about how he had married a Vietnamese woman and lived much of his life in Vietnam, working for a church agency to do relief and development work after the war. Vietnam had indeed shaped a significant part of his life. But he knew from being a pastor in Philadelphia that Vietnam had also affected veterans who lived on the streets and children of veterans who grew up with alcoholic fathers.

Vietnam had shaped a whole generation who went to college and became radicalized by "the movement." I thought about Fred's generation, and I wondered what 9/11 would mean for mine. If it meant war for America, how many young people my age would fight? Would there be a draft? Would people resist? And what would the church say? How would 9/11 shape the way we read the story of Jesus and think about the church universal?

I already told the story of the trip that Leah and I made with Christian Peacemaker Teams to Iraq at the beginning of Gulf War II. That experience of God's love from people who were supposed to be our enemies is really what catapulted us into an experiment in new monasticism at Rutba House. Five years later, I'm beginning to think that Fred was right: 9/11 is the defining moment for our generation. For so many people, 9/11 inspired a renewed patriotism that demands sacrifice in the name of a war on terror. For others it is a symbol of cynicism about a government that lied to its citizens and started a war for control of oil in the Middle East. But for a growing wave of new monastics, 9/11 is the event that woke us from our sleep and opened our eyes to Jesus's way of peace. It has caused us to question our American way of life, interrogating the hidden violence that prompted such an eruption of anger. But more than that, Ground Zero has become a mental space where we can hear the gospel with new ears. In the imagined rubble of our lives that those crumbling towers produced, we've heard a call to rebuild the church—to imagine a new architecture for Christian life in America.

Not long ago I was reading Jean Leclercq's introduction to a collection of Bernard of Clairvaux's writings. Bernard led one of the most significant monastic renewal movements in medieval Europe, founding the Cistercian community at Clairvaux in Champagne. What really struck me when I was reading, though, was Leclercq's description of the new monastic movement Bernard led: "There were thousands of men, generally young, who left society and often a military career to take up the cloistered life. If to this number one adds the members of some 290 other Cistercian monasteries founded during Bernard's lifetime, one has some idea of the tremendous peace corps, with tens of thousands of members, that Bernard helped to establish. What architect of peace has played such a role in his century or in any other?"[1]

I believe new monastic communities are forming a similar kind of peace corps in North America today. This peace army not only does battle with the weapons of the Spirit but is also calling the church in a time of war to remember that, whatever our politics, we are a body of peacemakers. We wage peace against the power of death because we have been given Jesus's life—a life of peace in which the dividing walls of hostility are already dismantled. If the church is to be good news for a generation whose defining moment is 9/11, we'll have to learn not only how to work for peace but also how to be God's peace in a world of conflict. New monastic communities may be one place to learn peaceful practices and forms for faithfulness in such a time as this.

Interrupting a Violent World

I like how the book of Ephesians talks about Jesus as our peace:

> For he is our peace; in his flesh he has made both groups into one and has broken down the dividing wall, that is, the hostility between us. He has abolished the law with its commandments and ordinances, that he might create in himself one new humanity in place of the two, thus making peace, and might reconcile both groups to God in one body through the cross, thus putting to death that hostility through it. So he came and proclaimed peace to you who were far off and peace to those who were near; for through him both of us have access in one Spirit to the Father. (Eph. 2:14–18)

1. Jean Leclercq in *Bernard of Clairvaux: Selected Works*, trans. G. R. Evans (New York: Paulist, 1987), 17.

Ephesians says that Jesus came preaching peace—that he *is* our peace, even—in a world fractured by violence. That is good news to people who have felt the pain of death and destruction. After all, not many people are proviolence. Pacifists who insist that violence is not necessary call war a tragedy. Generals who have led armies into battle agree that war is hell. Almost anyone who has seen violence longs for some balm to heal the wound that it exposes. The peace of Christ has been a comfort to young men in foxholes, mothers back at home, conscientious objectors sitting in prison, and martyrs who refused to fight. Our violent world aches in anticipation of the kingdom of peace that it was made for. That Jesus came preaching peace is good news for all of us.

But Ephesians gives more than a word of comfort. It is also a radical challenge to any church, no matter how progressive we may be on issues of war and peace. Because Ephesians doesn't just say that Jesus is our peace and that he'll make everything work out all right in the end. Ephesians claims that God has already broken down the dividing walls of hostility and created a place called church where peace is possible. His purpose was to "create in himself one new humanity in place of the two, thus making peace." Christ's body, the church, is a real place where God has made it possible for enemies to become one people, a new humanity in the world. That's what Ephesians is saying. And it's an incredible claim all by itself. But that's not all. There's more. Ephesians goes on to say, "And might reconcile both groups to God through the cross, thus putting to death that hostility through it." It's not just that God has made peace possible between enemies in the church. Participating in this peace, Ephesians says, is the one way people can be reconciled to God. In the one body where we live together with our former enemies, there is salvation. Outside of this fellowship, we cannot have a relationship with God.

The first time I ever sat and thought about this passage of scripture seriously, it scared me to death. In one sentence the Bible seems to say two things that almost none of us believe (this is especially frightening when you believe that all scripture is inspired by God). The first is this: peace with people who hate us really is possible in the church. It's not just some future hope, something that might happen if we work at it long enough or pray hard enough. No, Ephesians says it has already happened. Jesus has already broken down the dividing walls of hostility. Frankly, that's hard to believe. Especially if you've ever been part of a church. I grew up in a church that my family had to leave because the pastor got mad at my dad over an argument they had on the deacons' committee. How could *that* be the answer to the hostility between Al Qaeda and the West, Iraq and America?

While you're thinking about the answer to that question, let's go ahead and face up to what has to be the most frightening thing about this passage: Ephesians doesn't just say that peace with our enemies is possible. It says that peace with our enemies is the only way we can have peace with God. Believe me, I've tried to read it differently. I've looked at the Greek and I've done all the hermeneutical gymnastics I can imagine. I've wanted Ephesians to say something else, but I'm afraid that's what it says. You can't have peace with God outside the church that is God's peace. There is no personal relationship with Jesus without a personal relationship with your enemies.

I grew up in the South, albeit as a post–civil rights white boy who was oblivious to racial divisions. Without knowing it, I assumed the dividing wall of hostility called race. Only later did I learn the history that made my people the enemy of black folks. Take, for example, this story from North Carolina, my home state. In the fall of 1898, after the Civil War and federal reconstruction of the South, the *News and Observer* (still the main newspaper in our state) ran as the headline on its front page, "The Negroes Shall No Longer Rule North Carolina." Fueled by fear of a political alliance between poor blacks and whites, the publisher of the paper printed racist propaganda about black men raping white women and challenged all white men to defend the honor of their women. In Wilmington, North Carolina, white men stormed the streets, burning down black-owned businesses and attacking every black man in sight. At the end of the day, at least twenty-five black men lay dead, along with the political hopes of black folks for generations to come.[2]

For many of us raised in the post–civil rights era, stories like this are hard to believe. Where does that kind of hatred come from? I grew up knowing that white folks lived in King, North Carolina, and black folks lived in Walnut Cove. That's just the way it was. I didn't think we had any reason to hate each other. It would be nice to think that outbursts like the Wilmington Race Riot were anomalies, that they somehow reflected a normal peace gone bad. But the story is far too common for that to be the case. If you look long enough, there's a story like that of the Wilmington Race Riot in almost every Southern town.

In Atlanta it happened just eight years after Wilmington, in the Atlanta Race Riot of 1906. The results were almost the same as in Wilmington. Stirred up by rumors and propaganda in the papers, white mobs stormed the streets, sending black folks into hiding. Once again, at least twenty-five black men were killed. The impact on the social consciousness of both black and white Atlantans was immeasurable. W. E. B. Du Bois, who rushed home when he heard news of the riots to guard his home with a double-barreled shotgun, wrote in his "Litany at Atlanta":

> A city lay in travail, God our Lord, and from her loins sprang twin [sic] Murder and Black Hate. Red was the midnight; clang, crack and cry of death and fury filled the air and trembled underneath the stars when church spires pointed silently to Thee. And all this was to sate the greed of greedy men who hide behind the veil of vengeance!
> *Bend us Thine ear, O Lord!*

> In the pale, still morning we looked upon the deed. We stopped our ears and held our leaping hands, but they—did they not wag their heads and leer and cry with bloody jaws: Cease from

---

2. Michael Kazin, *A Godly Hero: The Life of William Jennings Bryan* (New York: Anchor, 2007), 205–6.

Crime! The word was mockery, for thus they train a hundred crimes while we do cure one.

Turn again our captivity, O Lord!

Behold this maimed and broken thing; dear God, it was an humble black man who toiled and sweat to save a bit from the pittance paid him. They told him: Work and Rise. He worked. Did this man sin? Nay, but some one told how some one said another did—one whom he had never seen nor known. Yet for that man's crime this man lieth maimed and murdered, his wife naked to shame, his children, to poverty and evil.[3]

In Atlanta today it is not just social convention or cultural preference that separates white from black, rich from poor. White and black are separated by a dividing wall of hostility because of a history of violence.

But not everywhere in Atlanta. 910 Ponce de Leon Avenue, home of the Open Door community in Atlanta, is an interruption to the status quo of the South. In some sixty rooms of a former women's mission, white and black folks live together as brothers and sisters in God's family. Peter Gathje describes the scene:

On the one hand, for those who come from the streets and prisons, the Open Door attempts to become a home where wounds inflicted by the streets and prisons can be healed and persons can be restored to their full human dignity. After years of surviving based on mistrust and hustling, this process requires continuous effort by all involved.

On the other hand, for those who come to the community from positions of power and privilege—who enter from the back door, there is also the need for healing and conversion from individualism, fear, desires for control, self-righteousness, and superiority. Deep faith in the redemptive power of love known in Christ, willingness to learn from each other, to hear correction of faults, and to have a sense of humor are some of

3. W. E. B. Du Bois, "Litany at Atlanta," available at www.harvardsquarelibrary. org/poets/dubois.php.

the ingredients the community has found necessary to build the circle of reconciliation among people from different backgrounds and experiences. Joining the circle requires God's gracious love and a willingness to be receptive to the transforming power of God's love.[4]

Together in community, people whose histories have shaped them to be enemies eat dinner together. They do it because they believe God has prepared a table for them—a space where they can indeed share the bread of life. Not that it's always easy, or that they always get it right. White and black folks at Open Door will be the first to tell you that they're not saints. They hurt one another, they fail to love, they sin against God like all of us. But they have an open door and a table where all are welcome, because they believe that Jesus is our peace and that the dividing wall of hostility has been knocked down, even when we act like it isn't or pick up the broken pieces to throw them at one another. "The difference between the Open Door and society," says cofounder Ed Loring, "is not in the presence or absence of sin and iniquity, but in our response to its presence and power in our lives."[5]

This is the lesson that new monastic communities have learned about peacemaking over and over again: we want to be the change we seek, but we soon realize that we're just as violent as the people we want to pacify. This would be cause for despair, except that we don't put our hope in the peace that we can make but in the peace God has already made with us through Jesus Christ. As Martin Luther said, the same word that kills also gives life. It is, at first, a terrifying thing to hear that the only way we can be reconciled with God is by becoming friends with our enemies. But once we trust God and begin to live in the new reality of a world without dividing walls, the struggles we go through in trying to live peaceably with one another become more than frustrating obstacles to a

4. Peter R. Gathje, *Sharing the Bread of Life: Hospitality and Resistance at the Open Door Community* (Atlanta: Open Door Community, 2006), 102.
    5. Ibid., 247–48.

peacemaking program. Instead, they are the substance of our faith—a concrete reminder of our vocation to "work out your own salvation with fear and trembling" (Phil. 2:12). Because the Jesus who is our peace is risen from the dead, we know that our struggle is not in vain. Sure, living with enemies can feel like death itself. But we are saved by the same power that raised Jesus from the dead.

Getting in the Way

When communities of disciples interrupt a violent world by living into God's peace with one another, it is inevitable that they will bump up against the culture of death around them. Like my granny used to say, "You don't have to pick a fight with the devil. Just live right, and he'll come after you." Or, to say it a little differently, what new monastic communities have found is that when you start walking in Jesus's way of peace you inevitably get in the way of the death-dealing powers in this world. This can be frightening, since no one wants to die. The ultimate threat of the principalities and powers is always, "Do as you're told or we'll kill you." But the Bible says, in a voice of resistance, "The fear of the LORD is the beginning of knowledge" (Prov. 1:7). It's scary to look death in the face, but it's even more frightening to imagine life outside the body where we are reconciled with God through the crucified flesh of Jesus. From the outside looking in, some journalists and preachers have praised new monastics, calling us courageous in our attempts to follow Jesus and find our way. I'm not trying to knock my friends or pretend a false humility, but on the whole I wouldn't say that new monastics are an exceptionally courageous lot. But we are, at our best, more afraid of God than we are of bombs, handguns, terrorists, or prison guards. When caught between allegiance to God and obedience to the authorities, we've tried to side with the One who created the heavens and puts rulers in their place.

Here in North Carolina, the Nazareth House offers hospitality to family members of men on Death Row at Raleigh's Central

Prison. Almost every week, mothers and brothers and aunts and cousins come and stay at Nazareth, telling their stories around the dinner table. Often when a man is executed, family members who have never been to see him during his imprisonment will come to say their last goodbyes and stay all week. Watching a family go through that week with their loved one feels strangely like living through Holy Week. By mandate of North Carolina statute, the prisoner is served a last supper on Thursday night, strapped to a gurney on Friday morning, and executed before a small gathering of witnesses. It's an agonizing process, through which our friends at Nazareth House stand with a prisoner's family, weeping, mourning, and praying to God for mercy.

In December 2005, after observing this rite numerous times with people whose stories we knew from friends at Nazareth House, a group of Christian peacemakers from six different new monastic communities in North Carolina came together to ask what we should do. We knew there were victims' rights activists, many of them Christian, who supported the death penalty as a just punishment for violent criminals. We also knew death penalty protestors, some of them Christian also, who argued against the death penalty because it disproportionately targets poor and black criminals and is an embarrassment to Western democracy. What we were most struck by, however, was the way the execution rite mimics Christ's passion in this Bible-belt state, almost as if the salvation of the people depends on this human sacrifice. The problem with the death penalty, we started saying, is that it forces us as citizens to participate in idolatry. We wanted people to know that Jesus died once and for all so that no one else would have to. More than anything, we didn't want to participate in the idolatry any longer.

So on the night when the state was scheduled to execute Kenneth Lee Boyd, the one thousandth person to be executed in the United States since the death penalty was reinstated in 1976, fifteen of us went in sackcloth and ashes, knelt before the prison, and blocked the entrance to prevent the witnesses from entering the building. Without witnesses, we knew, the execution could not go forward. In a matter of minutes we were arrested, and the execution continued. The next time an execution was scheduled, the police put up barricades to prevent us from entering the prison from a sidewalk. So we processed through the intersection in front of the prison singing, "Were you there when they crucified my Lord?" and held a worship service, honoring our Savior who laid down his life as a ransom for many. Again we were arrested and held in jail until the execution was completed. After we had done this a couple of times, the district attorney in Wake County convinced the magistrate to assign us five thousand dollars' bail. I spent the night in jail, waiting for a bench judge to let me out the next afternoon on a promise to appear for my court date.

After more than six months and a total of sixty-five arrests at four different executions, we finally had our day in court. The state presented its case, presenting aerial photographs and testimony from our arresting officers and the commander on duty to establish that we had indeed trespassed on prison property. We agreed that all those facts were true but told the judge that we wanted to offer in our defense an argument for the necessity of our actions. He invited me to take the stand and asked me to summarize our case. I told the judge that we were Christians and that we could not support state-sponsored executions that expressly mimic Christ's passion. I told him our Christian convictions compel us to take direct action to prevent any murder. We had trespassed at the prison to prevent a murder that we believed to be unjust and idolatrous.

"Before we proceed," the judge asked, "could you tell me how you read Romans 13?" I knew there was hope if the judge wanted to talk about the Bible. So I quoted for him Paul's injunction in Romans 13 to "submit to earthly authority" and said that we had learned from Martin Luther King that when a law is unjust in this country, it is the Christian's responsibility to break it and thereby bring it before a court that can evaluate its justice. "We are here today, Your Honor, to submit to your authority and ask for a decision about the justice of the death penalty." The judge nodded and asked us to present our case.

On the stand we talked about our relationships with people on Death Row and their family members. We explained that we had exhausted every legal means to try to stop the execution of the four men whose executions we had ultimately tried to prevent by trespassing. But more than anything, we talked about Jesus and the good news that all human sacrifice was brought to an end at the cross. The prosecutor asked if we had shared our faith with the prisoners before they were executed, and we said we had. As a matter of fact, all four of the men had been fellow Christians. "Doesn't Paul say, 'To be absent from the body is to be present with the Lord?'" he asked. I was on the stand at the time and gladly took the opportunity to explain that neither Jesus nor Paul preached a salvation of the soul apart from the body. The Romans crucified Jesus's body, but God raised his soul and his body from the dead. I said I knew I was just a preacher in a public courtroom, but I'd come to preach salvation of the whole person.

After my testimony as to our convictions and intentions, we asked the judge if we could call theologian Stanley Hauerwas as an expert witness. The judge hesitated, but we said we thought the court should hear from an expert on church doctrine whether there was any merit to our case. "Well, since he has come and waited so patiently, I'll let him take the stand," the judge said. Dr. Hauerwas explained to the judge the strong position against capital punishment that Pope John Paul II held, together with most of the major teachers of the church. "After all, the State executed our Lord," Hauerwas said. "The church has always had a problem with capital punishment." He went on to recount for the judge a history of Christian civil resistance to slavery, Jim Crow laws, foreign war, and nuclear armament. "This is what Christians do when their convictions run up against the systems of this world," he said. "They get in the way."

With that, we rested our case and waited for the judge's verdict. He began by saying that one of his early mentors had advised him that it was not wise to speak at any length from the bench. Generally he followed that advice. But he wanted to diverge in this case to say both that he admired our courage and that he was honored to hear this case in his courtroom. It was not in his power, however, to decide on the justice of the death penalty. He said that his job was simply to rule as to whether we were guilty of trespassing, and we had agreed that we were. So he found us guilty but suspended any sentence.

We walked out of the courtroom knowing that the judge had done all he could—if he wanted to keep his job, that is. A lawyer who had been following the death penalty in North Carolina for years congratulated us and said he didn't think executions would last another year. Less than six months later, the North Carolina Medical Board issued a statement saying that it would be a breach of medical ethics for any physician to participate in an execution. The state's protocol mandates that a physician be present for an execution to take place. The result has been a de facto moratorium on the death penalty in North Carolina.

One of the things we've learned from trying to stand in the way of a death-dealing system is that you can't do it alone. It takes a community. Plow Creek Community is a great example of this. If you visited their farm in rural Illinois, about two hours from Chicago, you might think they've fled from the world for a simple life, leaving behind any concerns of international politics. But you wouldn't have to stay long to hear from Jim Fitz and Erin Kindy about their work with Christian Peacemaker Teams in Colombia, Chiapas, and the West Bank. Plow Creek operates as a home base, sending them out to do direct-action peacemaking in conflict zones around the world. While they are away, fellow community members pray for them and care for their families. After each tour they come home to a place of peace and healing, where they tell the stories of what they have seen and heard.[6]

As new monastic communities have tried to walk in Jesus's way of peace during a time of war, we've heard more and more

6. To learn about the work of Christian Peacemaker Teams, visit www.cpt. org.

from soldiers. Disturbed by their experiences in the field, many of them have resonated with stories we've told about the people of Iraq. They have written e-mails from the field, sent letters, and even showed up at our door while home on furlough. Recently a friend at a community in the Northeast told me about a fellow who showed up at their house. While marching in formation at boot camp, this young soldier had heard the Lord saying, "Put down your gun." Not knowing what to do, he stepped out of formation and asked his sergeant if he could speak to him. The sergeant blew up, ripped the flags off his uniform, and humiliated him in front of the whole group. At his first chance, the soldier slipped away and hailed a cab, asking the driver to take him to the Greyhound station. "Now, I'm not saying that you *are* AWOL," the middle-aged woman told him, "but I'm just saying that if you *were*, you'd want to know that there are people stationed at the Greyhound station to pick you up. So I'm not saying that you are, but guys who want to get away usually ask me to take them by the Wal-Mart to buy a change of clothes." This soldier had followed her instructions, caught the next bus out of town, and found his way to a new monastic community.

As we have listened to the stories of soldiers, our communities have realized that it's not enough to get in the way of violence. More than that, we have to help these young people find a way to live that doesn't require them to sacrifice their bodies and their souls for a paycheck. An authentic antiwar movement can't be based on protest marches. We've heard Jesus calling us to direct action—not only to stop killing but also to create spaces where new life is possible for people who don't want to kill. In many of our neighborhoods, ROTC scholarships have been the only way most kids could go to college. To sign on with the army has been the best advice our churches could offer to young men who wanted to stay out of prison and off the streets. But communities of hospitality that are willing to welcome young men and women for a few months or years make it possible for them to "just say no" when Uncle Sam says "We want you." Of course, these are small acts of resistance to a huge power. Our recruiting dollars are nothing compared to what the U.S. Army invests in winning people for its cause.[7] But every building is built one brick at a time. Weak as it may look, God says that his kingdom will grow until it becomes a mountain that fills the whole earth (Dan. 2:35). The motley crew of a new peace corps that supports both active peacemakers and conscientious objectors may be a sign of hope for these troubled times.

Every Church a Peace Church

Unfortunately, peacemaking in North America has been the niche vocation of the so-called historical peace churches and the political left. This has resulted in two tragedies: on the one hand, a majority of Christians in the United States have little sense that Jesus is offering good news to them when he says, "Blessed are the peacemakers, for they will be called children of God" (Matt. 5:9). On the other hand, some peace churches and peace activists have focused so much on their important peace work that they haven't received the gift of adoption into God's shalom. So evangelical youth groups raise money by selling "Support Our Troops" bumper stickers. And Quakers feel more at home with Marxists than they do with brothers and sisters in Christ. Meanwhile, the world is not very much impressed by the good news of peace that the Bible proclaims.

When 9/11 happened and the United States declared a war on terror, I was working as a writer on faith and politics for a pretty conservative Christian think tank, the Institute for Global Engagement. I had lots of questions about Christian support for the war, but I could not write off the good and

7. Not long ago I saw a display in the local library where the U.S. Army was giving away a video war game to recruit young people. I called the recruiting officer and asked for a meeting. When I told him how shocked I was that he was using a game to entice young people to fight, he told me flatly that the army's research indicated that this was the most effective means of reaching people in their late teens and early twenties. Lord, have mercy.

honest people I worked with who believed that America had to defend itself. I spent a lot of time reading what has been written on war and peace in the Christian tradition, while also interviewing advocates of pacifism and just war. The most important thing I learned is that the just war and pacifist traditions are in agreement about the vocation of the church: we are called together in Christ's body for the peace of the world. Just war criteria give the church a language to use when talking with ruling authorities about the limits of war. But even those conversations are meant to be for the sake of peace. If Jesus Christ is indeed the peace of the world, then every church is called to be a peace church as his body. Differences about politics in the United States ought not to distract us from that primary vocation.

But white Christians in the West have inherited a sense of responsibility for the actions of our nation-states. In many ways it's hard for us to think about our vocation to be peacemakers as Christians because we can't see the difference between citizenship and church membership. Maybe not all U.S. citizens are Christian (it is a free nation, after all), but we assume that church membership will make us good citizens. When it doesn't, we're likely to question the authenticity of our Christian experience.

But this makes a lot of the New Testament seem out of place. If Christianity makes people good citizens of the worldly political system they live under, you have to wonder why Paul wrote most of his letters from prison and Jesus was executed by the ruling authorities. A serious reading of the Old and New Testaments seems to suggest that ever since Abraham, God has been calling people together to offer a political alternative to the kingdoms of this world. Of course God's people can work with the authorities that God permits to rule this world, especially when they seek justice and shun the pride that power breeds. Daniel served King Nebuchadnezzar, perhaps the most powerful man of his day. But he also reminded Nebuchadnezzar (on more than one occasion) that he was not God; when the king's decree conflicted with the law of God, Daniel and his friends disobeyed the king, at risk of their lives. But God used Daniel to invite even the emperor of Babylon into the peace of God's kingdom.[8]

I heard a story this Easter season of a church in a major U.S. city that decided to hold its Good Friday service in the federal building downtown. On this day when Christians traditionally fast, repent of our sins, and remember the death of Jesus, this body of believers remembered the deaths of Iraqi children and U.S. soldiers in the lobby of the federal building. They remembered how the world went dark and the earth shook on that Friday when Jesus was crucified. And they knew, as Christians, that they couldn't worship that Christ without somehow interrupting business as usual in their city. Wherever we gather and worship, the church must find ways to remember that what we are doing is an interruption—a celebration of the peace that God has given us right in the midst of a violent world.

If the peace of Christ really is an alternative to this world's violence, churches ought to get serious about putting it into practice. I like what Evangelicals for Social Action president Ron Sider has called for recently in his article "It's Time to Live What We Preach":

> Christian leaders (both just war and pacifist) from all traditions should together issue a call for something that has never happened yet in our history: the training and deployment of 10,000 to 25,000 CPT-type peacemakers who are committed to using the nonviolent teachings of Gandhi and King in unjust violent settings around the world. It would only take a few tens of millions of dollars. (Annual income of Christians is over 15 trillion dollars, so money is not the problem!) . . .
>
> If Christians mean what they have been saying for centuries about war and peace, then they have no choice. Without much planning and training, nonviolence has worked. It's time to invest $50 million in serious training and deployment. We cannot know ahead of time what will happen. But we already

8. Daniel 4 is Nebuchadnezzar's personal testimony of what he learned about the God of Israel. It's well worth a read. Try to imagine a president of the United States—or any other country, for that matter—telling a story like this one while in office.

know that unless we do this, our rhetoric about just wars and pacifism has been hypocritical and dishonest.[9]

A concerted effort to invest in peacemaking would go a long way toward making real the alternative that Jesus taught and practiced. But even more than this, a church that recognizes its vocation as the embodiment of God's peace has to invest in the things that make for peace. That is, we have to imagine a good and workable life for people that doesn't require violence.

A couple of years ago I spoke at a Baptist church in a military town about Jesus's way of peace and the life that God has made possible. It was a black church, and the audience was pretty sympathetic. But afterward I met a young white woman with two children whose husband was serving in Iraq. She was a guest at the church who had come because she'd heard someone was talking about Christian peacemaking. She talked about how difficult it was to think every day that her husband might die in a war that he shouldn't be fighting. She said her husband wanted out but that he couldn't find a way. Though the Army will grant conscientious objector (CO) status to people who object to any and every war, they won't do it for Christians who have reason to believe the particular war they are asked to fight is unjust. So only principled pacifists can get CO status. But the worst thing about it, this wife and mother told me, was that her church had no place for a military family that believes the war in Iraq is wrong. Her family was shunned by their church because they were unpatriotic and had too many doubts.

What the world needs more than anything is a church that will embrace families like this one who believe what the just war tradition has always taught—that there are times when Christians must say no to the war-making of ruling authorities (even when those authorities are one's boss). That kind of welcome is possible only when we are clear as Christians that allegiance to God trumps the claims of "Mars, Mammon, and

9. Ron Sider, "It's Time to Live What We Preach," available at www.esa-online. org/Display.asp?Page=home.

Me."[10] A church that has room for such resisters can become a sign to the world that we are not damned to a global struggle for power in which the last man standing will stand alone. God's peace is possible because God has made space for small acts of resistance right now—even in a military town.

10. Reba Place Fellowship in Evanston, Illinois, uses this little formulation to name three of the most potent powers and principalities of our age. As of August 2007, the good folks there have been striving to resist these powers by the grace of God for fifty years.

8

A CULTURE OF GRACE AND TRUTH

John's Gospel begins by claiming that we have seen the glory of God in Jesus, "the glory as of a father's only son, full of grace and truth" (John 1:14). That was a pretty incredible thing for a Jew to say in the first century. If John had gone to the rabbi at his local synagogue, the rabbi would have told him that no mortal could survive the sight of God's glory. John might have argued that Moses had a chance to see the backside of God, but he would have had to acknowledge that there is a considerable difference between seeing someone's glory and seeing their backside. And Moses only told the people about that sight later. God's people in the first century just didn't believe that is was possible to see God's glory in this life.

Two thousand years later, it may be that little has changed. If you went to the pastor at your local church today and asked about the distinctive mark of Jesus's followers, odds are she could quote for you John 13:34–35: "I give you a new commandment, that you love one another. Just as I have loved you, also should you love one another. By this everyone will know that you are my disciples, if you have love for one another." But if you started looking for that kind of community, full of grace and truth, you might start to think that you're just as likely to find God walking around in human skin. In most any church you could probably find a few folks who love selflessly and shine like stars with the gentle glory of God made flesh. (I've had the privilege of knowing a few of these people myself.) But you'd have to admit that there's a significant difference between a handful of shining saints and a new community where people love one another as God loves the world. Jesus said his glory would shine forth in the church's new culture of grace and truth. But for most of us in the United States, it's hard to imagine seeing that in this life.

Now I don't want to overstate the case. The Bible also teaches, after all, that human beings are broken by sin. So it ought not surprise us when people can't get along or when nearly everyone just does what they have to do to take care of themselves. Cain killed his own brother (which is always worth noting when people advocate for the ideal of "one human family"). Even Jesus said there would be "wars and rumors of wars." The Bible doesn't teach us to expect a world where everybody naturally loves and respects everyone else. But Jesus does tell his disciples to "love one another." And Jesus seems to think that the Holy Spirit will enable members of his body to do that. Indeed, that's how Jesus says other people will know that there is good news for the world—because a church exists where people genuinely love one another. It's a little scary to say it, but I think John Howard Yoder was right when he said, "Where Christians are not united, the gospel is not true in that place."[1]

So for those of us who believe that the gospel is the hope of the world, it's worth asking how united our churches are. Sadly, unity with fellow Christians may be the point at which it's hardest to be a Christian in North America. And it's not just because our churches seem to be willing to split over practically any disagreement that can't be settled in the foreseeable future. Our impatience itself may be a sign that we haven't

1. John Howard Yoder, *The Royal Priesthood: Essays Ecclesiastical and Ecumenical*, ed. Michael Cartwright (Scottsdale, PA: Herald, 1998), 291.

yet heard the good news. Which is a pretty scary thought, in and of itself. But I appreciate Yoder's precision with language. "Where Christians are not united," he says, "the gospel is not true *in that place*." That's very different from saying that the gospel is not true. Because if it's not true only *in a particular place*, that means something must be wrong with the place, not with the gospel. And if the problem is with the place or time or people, things could always change to make the gospel true there also. The gospel is good news because it promises the possibility of a whole new world.

But the big question is, how do we get from where we are to the world that we were made for? In the context of an Empire, it may well be that all roads lead to Rome. But the kingdom Jesus announced is peculiar not only in its vision of a new creation, but even more so in the way God chooses to get us there. We can't just get our vision from scripture and make it happen however works best. Sure, unity is what we're called to. But church unity isn't something we can achieve through clever negotiations, the force of authority, or even the patience of waiting our enemies out. There's only one way to Christian unity: we embody the grace and truth of Christ's glory when we love one another as God has already loved us. Truth is, that hasn't sounded very interesting to our churches for a long time.

Grassroots Ecumenism

Not that there hasn't been plenty of talk about the need for unity in American churches. Pick up any book on the history of the church in the West, turn to the twentieth century section, and you'll inevitably find "Ecumenical Movement" in bold type with a whole section devoted to it. Of course, if you're reading a more conservative American church history, that section might explain why ecumenism is bad. Despite the best of intentions, it turns out that even the ecumenical movement was a conversation only among certain mainline denominations. A little bit of history helps explain that.

Early in the twentieth century, U.S. Christians argued heatedly in what historians now call the fundamentalist-modernist controversy. While the issues were (and still are) complex, the debate came to be symbolized dramatically in the so-called Scopes Monkey Trial. William Jennings Bryan, perhaps the most famous preacher in the country at the time, was called in by the district attorney's office in small-town east Tennessee to prosecute John Scopes, a little-known high school teacher who had accepted an invitation from the American Civil Liberties Union to challenge legislation against teaching evolution as scientific fact in public schools. Bryan, a progressive reformer who advocated for women's suffrage, preached against imperial war-making, and resisted corporate control of public life, had also mounted a campaign against the theory of evolution. He claimed that he was obligated to do this as a Christian for two reasons. First, he thought evolution contradicted scripture, which says God created human beings in his own image. Second, and equally important for Bryan, teaching evolution as fact would inevitably lead to social Darwinism, where the poor and needy whom Christ had blessed would be deemed unfit for survival because they were an impediment to human progress.

Bryan is a good example of the sort of Christianity that was possible in the United States before the fundamentalist-modernist controversy. Without seeing any contradiction, he held together progressive politics and a conservative reading of scripture. But Bryan dropped dead just after the Scopes trial, and the nation has remembered him as a symbol of fundamentalist literalism. After the Scopes trial in 1920, Christians felt increasingly pulled by the political forces in America to choose between biblical literalism and liberal politics.[2]

2. Michael Kazin, *A Godly Hero: The Life of William Jennings Bryan* (New York: Anchor, 2007); see especially the final chapter. Kazin's very good biography of Bryan helped me to see how it was possible to be a literalist and a liberal in the United States before the Scopes trial. But I'm not saying that we need to go back to nineteenth-century evangelicalism. Even if the church is able to hold together the left and right of U.S. politics, that's not necessarily the same thing as embodying a kingdom "not of this world." The politics of Jesus, it seems, is more radical than we've even begun to imagine.

Those who chose liberal politics ended up in what we now call the mainline denominations.[3] These churches believed deeply in Christian responsibility for civic life, trusting that science and democracy were gifts from God to lead humanity into a new era of peace. They looked down on fellow Christians who questioned science and "secular humanism." So when mainliners decided to talk seriously about church unity in an ecumenical dialogue, some things were just assumed. For starters, they took it as a given that fundamentalists (and, later, evangelicals) wouldn't be included. But even more important, they assumed that the political dividing lines between them would stand. The ecumenical dialogue not only excluded some Christians; it also failed to question the political formation that had made the fundamentalist-modernist controversy so determinative in people's lives. Delegates to ecumenical meetings ended up looking and talking a lot like ambassadors to the United Nations.

Of course, it wasn't just the mainliners who settled into the political identity America gave them. Fundamentalists weren't any better at questioning these assumptions. They just stood their ground on the other side of the divide. While mainline denominations sent delegates to talk about differences in doctrine and try to find some common ground, conservative churches continued to split throughout the twentieth century, also over doctrinal issues (though different ones). The unifying center of fundamentalist Christianity increasingly became conservative politics. Especially after *Roe v. Wade*, churches that had split over debates about free will and the second coming of Christ found their common cause by voting for the Republican Party.

I'm not very interested in asking who was right and who was wrong in these debates, which by the time I was growing up had

3. Sometimes people hear "mainline" and think it just means "mainstream." But the word has an interesting history. The Mainline is a road that runs east out of Philadelphia where rich folk built big homes outside the city. The Presbyterian, Episcopal, and Methodist churches they built defined the culture of American Christianity's left wing. When I say mainliners felt "responsible" for society in the twentieth century, what I mean is they owned the businesses, ran the government, and called the shots.

turned into the "culture wars." I've met smart and respectable
Christians on both sides of the left-right divide in America.
My teacher Tony Campolo used to say, "When they ask if I'm
Republican or Democrat, I say, 'Name the issue.'" More and
more I hear from people who want to build a bridge across the
divides and work together for a better future.

But I see new monastic communities doing something a little
different. Rather than worry about restructuring U.S. politics,
we believe God has already made a different kind of politics
possible in the church. We've started trying to live in God's
kingdom where we are practicing—among other things—a
"grassroots ecumenism." We haven't figured out all the doctrinal issues that divide denominations. But Baptists have moved
in with Catholics, and folks who come from money share life
with people who used to be homeless. Billy Kenny at Communality in Lexington, Kentucky, often says that the most radical thing about that community's life is that Republicans and
Democrats eat together. They're able to do it because they've
been caught up into something more important than their
ideas about American politics. They've heard rumors of a new
political order that has broken into the world, offering the kind
of life that can go on forever—eternal life.

Sometimes when I talk with evangelical friends about the
grassroots ecumenism of new monastic communities, they tell
me I'm not taking doctrine seriously enough. I worry about
this myself (especially when I think someone I'm living with
is wrong). I worry not so much because I want to be right;
I worry because I don't want to see people I love destroyed
by lies. (I'm a writer and a preacher—a wielder of words, you
might say—because I'm convinced that what we think and
believe is a life-and-death issue.) But I believe Jesus died and
rose again so that we could have the time to live together, even
when we disagree. I know it may sound strange, but while
everyone else is rushing to prove their enemies wrong before
they wreck the world, Jesus has given us the gift of time to
wait together, knowing that someone else has already saved
the world.

What to Do When You Can't Save the World

All this talk about the gift of time can easily sound removed from reality, like an excuse to sit back and do nothing—especially when coming from a guy who has the time to write a book. But if you've read this far, I hope you'll trust that I'm not trying to retreat from good work. What I really want to name is the work that we most need to be doing—tending the good gift of a culture of grace. I don't know if I can convince you that God has already given us all the time we need to bear with one another, but if you'll give me a few minutes I'll tell you the story that convinced me. It's the story of a community called Antioch in Jackson, Mississippi.

When my friend Chris Rice was a student at Middlebury College in Vermont, John Perkins came to preach on his campus. A veteran of the civil rights movement and a pioneer of Christian community development, Perkins is also a persuasive preacher. He proclaimed the good news of relocation, redistribution, and reconciliation in Christ. After hearing him, Chris was compelled to take a break from Middlebury to spend a few months at Voice of Calvary, the church and community development ministry Perkins had started in Jackson, Mississippi. Chris arrived in Jackson eager to save the neighborhood. There he met Spencer Perkins, the founder's oldest son. Chris remembers the first words he ever heard Spencer say: "What are all you white people doin' here?"[4] Chris could not have imagined then that he would spend the next seventeen years of his life in Jackson and that Spencer would become his friend, fellow community member, and partner in ministry. He couldn't have imagined it because it was all a gift, given and received in time. That was something he and Spencer could only learn together.

Spencer's question about white motives sparked a racial crisis at the Voice of Calvary Church, a Deep South experiment in interracialism that stuck out in the early 1980s even more than

4. Chris Rice, *Grace Matters: A True Story of Race, Friendship, and Faith in the Heart of the South* (San Francisco: Jossey-Bass, 2002), 11.

it does today. The fallout from the crisis wasn't easy for anyone at the church, but it led the elders to start household groups where members would meet together for Bible study. Chris was assigned to Spencer's group. After hearing each person tell their own story, the group read through the Sermon on the Mount and asked what it would mean to take Jesus at his word. Their study eventually led them to Acts, where they read about how in the early church believers shared what they had in common and became a new kind of community (Acts 2:42–47). Though they knew from their histories that race, economics, and political differences divided them, the group decided that in Christ they could share a new life together. They bought two houses and moved in together, calling themselves Antioch after the church in Acts where believers were first called "Christian" because the old categories of Jew and Gentile didn't fit anymore.

Out of their life together in community, Chris and Spencer developed a national reconciliation ministry. They published *Urban Family* magazine, wrote a book together, and traveled around the country preaching the good news of unity in Christ. The only problem was that they couldn't get along with each other. And it wasn't just a personality conflict. Chris and Spencer knew one another well enough to know the other's deep brokenness. John Alexander, who became their teacher and counselor, described their relationship as a "mess." "Naturally, this was embarrassing," he wrote. "What's more, their conflicts had a lot to do with race. Which made it very embarrassing. Like marriage counselors filing for divorce. Or child psychologists with wretched kids." John listened to Chris and Spencer's complaints about one another and their confession that they were not worthy to speak about reconciliation. "Spencer and Chris were right, of course," John quipped. "They were unworthy. . . . They called Judy [John's wife] and me in, hoping we could fix them. Well, if I may say so myself, we failed. When we were done, they were still a mess. As we all are."[5]

5. John Alexander, "Stop Going to Church and Be the Church," manuscript, quoted with permission.

But in the midst of coming to terms with their own broken as individuals and as a community, the folks at Antioch learned the truth about God's grace. It was a real breakthrough—a lesson that made it possible for them to go on when they felt as if everything was falling apart. "I never understood until now that God intended for grace to be a way of life for his followers," Spencer wrote. "Sure, I knew that we are supposed to love one another as Christ loved us. But somehow it was easier to swallow the lofty untested notion of dying for each other than simply giving grace to brothers and sisters on a daily basis, the way God gives us grace."[6] John had told Chris, Spencer, and the folks at Antioch to stop trying to fix each other, because to the extent that any of us gets fixed, it happens only by grace. John was speaking from a lifetime of experience in Christian community, first at Jubilee Fellowship in Philadelphia and later at Church of the Sojourners in San Francisco. After more than ten years together, the folks at Antioch knew enough to trust that John was right. "That day John taught me what is enough," Chris says. "It is enough to get the love of God into your bones and to live as if you are forgiven. It is enough to care for each other, to forgive each other, and to wash the dishes. The rest of life, he taught me, was details."[7] It's not that there isn't work to be done—all the way down to the dishes. But grace means there is enough time and love and patience and forgiveness to bear with one another as we struggle to do the good work God has called us to do.

The Work of the Church Is Grace

New monastics aren't special people or super-Christians. If anything, we need intentional disciplines and a daily rhythm of prayer because we're more broken than most people. But on our best days, in life together at places like Antioch, we know that our work is to tend to a culture of grace and truth in the

6. Spencer Perkins, "Playing the Grace Card," *Christianity Today*, July 13, 1998, 44.

7. Rice, *Grace Matters*, 260.

world. That's hard for most of us to get our heads around, because we're used to troubleshooting and problem solving. But the work of the church is a kind of tending. The best analogy I know for it is gardening.

We have a garden at Rutba House, but I'll have to admit that I don't really get it. I show up for workdays every once in a while to chop weeds or dig a new bed. But I don't really understand gardening. Now, grocery shopping I get. You go to the store with a list of things you need, find them on the shelf, put them in your cart, pay at the checkout line, and come home with a meal. That whole process makes sense to me. But gardening is weird. You dig up your lawn, add in some compost, bury a seed, and all you've got at the end of the day is a strip of dirt in your yard. Seems like a lot of work for no immediate return. I've learned over time that there's always work to be done in a garden—pulling weeds, watering, staking up vines, running off groundhogs. But all of it is work that you do so that something else can happen—namely, growth. The crazy thing about a garden is that you're always working but there's nothing you can do to make it grow. In the end every garden is a miracle. Which is to say, it is a gift wrapped in mystery.

Best I can figure, community is a lot like a garden. Somehow there's always work to be done—dishes to wash, meetings to go to, prayers to pray, meetings to go to, laundry to wash, meetings to go to, meals to prepare . . . and more meetings to go to. After you've sat through a few hundred meetings and heard the same people say more or less the same things over and again, you are tempted to think, "I know what this community needs. If they would just listen to me, we could get on with more important things." But it never works. Because, as with a garden, you can't make community grow. All you can do is tend to a culture of grace and truth by listening to every voice, loving people who frustrate you, telling the truth as best as you can, and doing the dishes.

The great temptation in community is to imagine that our life together is not like a garden, but instead like a repair shop. In the repair shop cars are broken and need to get fixed. Normally cars run just fine on their own. As a matter of fact, that's what they're made to do. If you see one car pulling another on the highway, you know something went wrong. They're probably on the way to the repair shop. There are people at the repair shop who know a thing or two about cars. They figure out what's wrong, get the parts they need, tinker around under the hood, and fix it. That's the whole point of a repair shop. Bring 'em in. Name their problem. Fix it. Send 'em home.

Now I have to tell the truth: it doesn't take long in community to realize that people are broken and in need of repair. And the minute you realize this, you're liable to think, "I can name this person's problem much better than she can. And I know a thing or two about people. Maybe I can help fix her." You do this because you love her, of course, and you want to see her get better. You want to see her back on the road, doing the things she was made to do. The problem is, people aren't like cars. We aren't made to run just fine on our own. We're made for community.

Which means we need something more like a garden than a repair shop. Of course, plants get sick just as cars get broken. I'm not saying that you don't get broken people in community or even that some people aren't more broken than others. But I am saying that broken people need what sick plants need. They need someone to tend to the soil around them, give them some extra attention, pull the weeds that threaten to choke them, and wait. It turns out in the end, I think, that we all need that sometime or another. But the repair shop won't do, because we're made for life in a garden. And the only way to grow up into life in the garden is to get your roots in good and stay there.

Just as communities are tempted to become repair shops for people, we can also deceive ourselves into thinking that we're a repair shop for society. Much of what I've tried to say in this book is about how community is a social, political, and economic project, offering an alternative to the death-dealing systems of this world. And I believe that. It's not just that people are broken; society is broken too. We don't just have some sick plants. Our problem is bad soil, polluted and neglected by years of misuse. Like the gurus of modern agriculture who want to save the soil with pesticides and fertilizers, communities can become captivated by activism. We can spend ourselves on campaigns to make poverty history, end hunger, stop war, and promote reconciliation. Like the guys at the repair shop, we can say, "I understand the problem. I've got some resources and know-how. Maybe I can help fix it." But this is not the work of the church either. Because the world doesn't need a repairman. The world needs a Savior. And, thank God, we already have one. Paul says it like this to the church at Corinth: "If anyone is in Christ, behold—new creation! Old things are gone, the new has come!" (2 Cor. 5:17, my translation). Just as God planted a garden at the beginning of Genesis, there is a new garden in the world. With Jesus, something new has come. We can't fix bad soil and we can't repair broken plants, but the good news is we don't have to. Our work is to tend to the new creation that has already come, full of grace and truth. The good news is that's enough.

Fewer Services, More Service

So how does a congregation get the love of God deep in its bones and start tending to a culture of grace and truth among its people? One way to start is by paying more attention to church members. I want to propose a slogan: "Fewer Services, More Service." Most churches focus a great deal of energy each week on creating a meaningful worship experience. I have no objection to that. Worship is important. And when we do it right, worship helps to shape us into the image of God. But when we do it wrong, it's easy to start thinking that church is about going to worship services. There's Sunday morning worship and Sunday evening worship. Then Wednesday night prayer meeting can also end up looking a lot like one more worship service. As can Tuesday night's ministry at the nursing home, vacation Bible school, Thursday morning's prayer service, and Saturday's praise concert. Of course, some church services look less like worship and more like social services. In some congregations, the week is marked by services to the homeless, the hungry, the poor, and the addicted. But all of these services are also events that members go to or staff offer to the community. Unfortunately, very little energy is put into helping members know one another well enough that they could tend to a culture of grace and truth in their midst.

But note that the service Jesus offered on the night he taught his disciples to love one another was a very mundane service *to them*. Jesus didn't invite them to a worship service. Nor did he create an opportunity for the disciples to serve the disadvantaged of Jerusalem. Instead, Jesus washed his disciples' feet. Then he said this: "So if I, your Lord and Teacher, have washed your feet, you also ought to wash one another's feet" (John 13:14). Now, a few churches I know of actually practice foot washing as a ritual. Some other churches have "Basin and Towel" ministries that serve the poor and needy in their communities. But I'm not so sure that Jesus was talking about either of those things when he said, "You also ought to wash one another's feet." Because washing feet wasn't a ritual in first-century Palestine. Nor was it an outreach ministry. Washing feet was the daily job of servants—people who tended to the basic needs of others in a household. Poor people presumably washed their own feet (or went without clean feet). But Jesus said the church would be the sort of place where each person would become the servant of everyone else. Jesus said the world will know we are his disciples if we love one another by tending to each other's basic needs.

I wonder how many people in churches actually know the basic needs of their fellow church members. For the most part it seems that Christians with resources pay someone else to cut their grass, cook their food, look after their children, clean their toilets, and wash their clothes (unless they particularly enjoy doing some of these things themselves or think it better to spend the money on something else). At the same time, poor Christians find themselves taking care of these basic needs for themselves (or watching them go unmet). We rarely talk about how we could meet one another's basic needs. It doesn't often occur to Christians that this is what church is about.

But if John's Gospel is right in suggesting that the glory of God is revealed in the world when believers tend to a culture of grace and truth by taking care of one another, then it seems churches should invest at least as much energy into organizing service to one another as we put into worship services and social services. The ministry of organizing childcare co-ops and shared meals, lending lawnmowers and scrubbing floors is every bit as important as preparing a sermon or working the soup line. And it doesn't make any more sense to pretend that we can take care of each other through "random acts of kindness" than it does to imagine that preachers can proclaim good news through random inspiration. Washing feet is real work. But it's work like gardening is work. We roll up our sleeves and do our best at it, knowing that there may not be much to show for our efforts at the end of the day. But that's OK, because beneath the surface, in ways that we can never completely understand, little miracles are happening. New life is taking root and breaking through to the surface. When we tend to one another, God's glory is revealed. And it looks like a culture of grace where people care enough about one another to speak the truth in love.

9

WHY NEW MONASTICS NEED THE CHURCH

Maybe the most important thing new monasticism has to say to the church is that we need it. We're not trying to leave the church behind and do something new on our own. No, we are children of the church. We dream of a kingdom of justice and peace because we were raised up on the story of God's people. We long for community because we've heard rumors of a new humanity. We remember the body and blood of Jesus in the bread and wine and broken pieces of a story that still compels us. We are finding our way with Jesus, and what we're finding is that we need the church.

It may be that this is the truly "new" thing God is doing through new monasticism. Community movements in U.S. history have often been inspired by Christianity and the church as it is described in the book of Acts. But it has been hard for community movements to maintain their connection to the church. The most recent example is the Jesus People movement of the 1970s, in which hundreds of new communities sprang up, promising a more radical commitment to the way of Jesus and a new society in its wake. A few of those communities are still around, but most of them are gone. As independent projects, cut off from the larger church and often focused on the leadership of a charismatic figure, they ran out of energy and died. The ones that have survived have done so because they saw the need to stay connected to the church as it exists while continuing to ask what the church might become by God's grace. Jesus People USA, a community I've already mentioned that grew out of the Jesus People movement, was independent for a number of years but became part of the Evangelical Covenant Church a few years ago. They joined a denomination not because they think it's perfect, but because they've learned from experience that they need the church.

"The church is a whore," St. Augustine said, "but she's our mother." Even as we pray, "Our Father, who art in heaven," we need our mother here on earth to pass on her wisdom and keep us from one generation to the next. No, she's not perfect. But neither are we. The only way we know that is because our mother taught us to confess our sins. We need her more than we can know.

Becoming the Church

In the last chapter on a culture of grace and truth, I mentioned John Alexander, who was a teacher and counselor to Chris Rice, Spencer Perkins, and the whole community at Antioch at a time when they needed to remember grace. John's own story is the best way I know to say why new monastics need the church. John was the son of a Conservative Baptist pastor who decided in the 1960s that taking scripture literally meant getting on the right side of the civil rights movement. So John and his father started a little magazine called *Freedom Now* (later *The Other Side*) to explain to Baptist pastors why they and their churches should get behind the movement for freedom and equality that their black brothers and sisters were leading. This did not make John many friends among evangelicals. He lost his teaching job at Wheaton College and found himself working more and more with "peace and justice" people who sympathized with the political left, whether they were Christian or not.

John was angry with fundamentalists for being racists and not believing that the gospel could overcome that. But after a number of years among liberals, he also became disappointed with them. They were not much better at loving one another than the fundamentalists with whom he'd grown up. As a matter of fact, John thought they were enslaved in the same ego game that everyone else was playing.

> My experience of Christians, including myself, has been that we are far from holy, and my experiences of churches and of Christendom at large have perhaps been even worse. A child of the sixties, I followed my generation in how I dealt with the problem: I didn't quite lose my idealism, but it morphed into judgmentalism, cynicism, negativity, skepticism, confusion.
>
> Most of my experience has been among evangelicals and fundamentalists. (My father was a fundamentalist Baptist preacher moving toward evangelicalism.) I was unimpressed by what I saw among his peers and concluded that something was missing from their lives. (Many of them were segregationists.) I thought there had to be something more. I have no doubt that I was too harsh on them, but neither do I have any doubt about there being something more.
>
> So I wandered in other pastures, among more liberal folk and more catholic folk. They were different from fundamentalists and evangelicals, usually in ways I preferred, but in those churches, I still found few reaching toward anything approximating holiness. Most of them lacked intensity about their faith—the intensity of my father and of many fundamentalists. This made them easier to be with (they were less fanatical!), but if the New Testament is anything, it's intense. It was hard to picture these sensible people following anyone as wild as the Jesus or Paul who actually appear in the New Testament. Once again something was missing. There had to be something more.
>
> So I wandered farther afield, among Christians and almost-Christians who were hippies and political radicals. I found a

pretty comfortable niche with them (they were intense), but
I eventually found their rights orientation (by then, *my* rights
orientation) to lack depth. (Their litany of who was violating
their rights and the rights of others grew boring and had a stun-
ningly different tenor from Jesus' teaching.) Besides, they were
no better than schismatic fundamentalists at getting along with
folks, and often their sexual stance was roughly as destructive
as nuclear war.

Again something was missing. I began to wonder (not without reason) whether the problem was me. Was I so negative
that I couldn't belong to anything that wasn't perfect (which
leaves rather few groups to belong to)? I began to suspect that
I was a homeless wanderer, a professional critic suffering from
terminal self-righteousness. That's undoubtedly the end point
of the postmodernism of my generation, and I didn't want it as
my end point. Something was really missing there.[1]

John didn't like the trajectory he was on. So he dropped out.
John left *The Other Side* magazine and his life on the speaking circuit. He left it all and moved to a little church community in California. John believed that God saved him in
that little church community. God saved his marriage and his
life—saved his soul, even. God saved John by making him part
of the church. He started saying that he thought God was calling us to "stop going to church and become the church." John
discovered that the church was meant to be an alternative to
the dead-end roads he'd wandered down with fundamentalists,
evangelicals, liberals, and radicals.

John had a way of summarizing what he had learned about
the church. He asked people to imagine a gang member. Call
him Jimmy. Say Jimmy has been running drugs for ten years
and is headed straight for prison or the grave. What does he
need? The fundamentalists John grew up with would say that
Jimmy needs a personal relationship with Jesus. And they
would be right. Jimmy needs a conversion experience and a
personal transformation to become the person God wants

1. This quote taken from personal papers of John Alexander. Used with
permission.

him to be. But if all Jimmy gets is a sinner's prayer and a
church to go to on Sunday mornings, he'll take his personal
relationship with Jesus right back with him to the gang. And
he'll go on living the same way he has been. So what do the
liberals say Jimmy needs? John said they may note that Jimmy
is a victim of racism along with his neighbors and they may
work hard to build a health clinic in his underserved community. And they would be right. Because if Jimmy stays in
the gang, he'll get shot and need someone to sew him up.
But after the doctor saves his life, he'll send Jimmy home to
the same gang. The doctor doesn't have anything more to
offer Jimmy.

"What Jimmy really needs," John would say at the end of this
thought experiment, "is a new gang." Jimmy needs new people
to go home to and make a life with. He needs to be part of a
people where he can have a personal relationship with Jesus
and a social order free of racism. But these commitments can't
be any more abstract than the concrete realities and relationships of a gang. The church is called to be a people who love
one another and make a life together, tending to a culture of
grace in a world broken by sin. The truth is that when we fail
to do that, we fail to be the church.

Parachurch vs. Prochurch

But it's hard to be a people who love each other. It's hard
because Christians disagree about so many things. If you actually take the time to talk things through with people who are
different from you, you begin to feel like you're never going
to get anything done. That's why U.S. Christians invented the
parachurch organization. "Alongside" churches but independent of them, parachurch organizations provide a space where
Christians can get things done "in Jesus's name." People who
agree on action can pool their resources to feed the hungry,
relieve disasters, save the planet, fight abortion, minister to
prisoners, or support their favorite political party. And if you

don't agree with some action, you don't have to send your monthly contribution to that organization.

But there's a problem: if parachurches are the place where we get the stuff done that we really care about, then church becomes less and less important. You might go to church because a worship service makes you feel good or because you need to maintain good relationships with donors. But church isn't really necessary. You could probably do without it.

When there are important things to get done and you know for certain that God is calling you to do them, church can seem like an unnecessary obstacle that gets in the way of discipleship. It's pretty easy to forget that church is the only way we know what discipleship means. More than that, it's possible to be a churchgoing Christian and never learn that church is God's tactic for defeating the powers of darkness in this world. That's what Ephesians 3:10 says: "So that through the church the wisdom of God in its rich variety might now be made known to the rulers and authorities in the heavenly places." The powers of darkness will not know that they are defeated because of evangelistic campaigns or ecumenical councils, nor through the peace movement or intentional community movements. Ephesians says that the principalities and powers will learn of their defeat through the gathering of believers in the world that we call church.

Peter Maurin, cofounder of the Catholic Worker, used to quip, "Movements don't move me." I know the feeling. If new monasticism is just a movement in American Christianity, it will move on and some other movement will follow, like waves rolling against the shore. When I look back at church history, though, I see something different in the monastic communities that have formed and developed on the margins of the church. These communities never claimed to be doing anything more than what they heard in the Bible that the church taught them. They knew all Christians were not necessarily called to live like them. But the monastics also knew that they were like every other Christian. They had been called from the stormy seas of this world into the ark of safety. However much it might stink inside, it was the only way to make it through this world alive. "Outside of the church there is no salvation" was not an assertion of power-hungry popes but a humble confession that, however odd it might seem, this was how God had decided to save the world.

So if new monasticism is a movement, I at least want to say that it's a *prochurch* movement. God only knows if our communities will last or if the practices that have given us life will be of some help to other Christians. I figure we don't really need to know what God will make of our little efforts in local places to hear Jesus and obey him. The good news is that God has already told us what we have to know—that, by grace, we're saved from ourselves and given new life in the church. We learn who we are in Christ as we find our way together. As Catherine of Siena said, "All the way to heaven is heaven because Jesus said, 'I am the Way.'"

School for Conversion (SFC) offers theological education and practical formation for the sake of conversion into a new way of life. Based in Christian communities of neo-monastic discipleship, SFC facilitates study directed toward the creation of new community and creative expressions of God's kingdom in the abandoned spaces of society. Courses include:

SFC 101: Intro to Christianity as a Way of Life

Jesus's announcement of the kingdom of God is an invitation to come and follow—to learn a whole new way of living. This course, hosted by new monastic communities, introduces students to the theology and practice of Christianity as a way of life in five sessions. *School(s) for Conversion: 12 Marks of a New Monasticism* (Cascade 2005) is the primary text for this course. Students stay with host community and are invited to participate in the community's common life for three days.

SFC 103: New Monasticism: What It Has to Say to Today's Church

Monasticism has always helped the church remember who she is. This course is designed to help local churches explore five practices that have emerged from new monastic communities: reading Scripture as the story of God's people, relocation to abandoned places, economic sharing, gospel peacemaking, and cultivating a culture of grace and truth. *New Monasticism: What It Has to Say to Today's Church* (Brazos, 2008) is the primary text for this course. It is hosted by local churches.

SFC 201: Christian Identity and the Mission of the Church in the Americas

This travel course is a short-term, immersion-learning experience in Argentina or Brazil. It is designed for university and seminary students, as well as other small groups (e.g., short-term missions and/or discovery trips for local churches) who are interested in a first-hand look at the challenges and possibilities for our understanding of world Christianity as both a global and local reality, taking the Latin American context as a "marker" for understanding Christian identity and mission in the Americas.

For more information and a schedule of upcoming course locations, visit:

www.newmonasticism.org/sfc

The Tradition Alive

" Brazos Press seeks to be faithful to the wide and deep embrace of God, publishing out of and to all the major streams of the historic Christian tradition. *"*

Brazos Press is grounded in the ancient, ecumenical Christian tradition, understood as living and dynamic. As legend has it, Brazos is the Spanish name explorers gave to a prominent Texas river upon seeing how its winding waters sustained fertile soil in an arid land. They christened this life-giving channel Los Brazos de Dios, "the arms of God."

Our logo connotes a river with multiple currents all flowing in the same direction, just as the major streams of the Christian tradition are various but all surging from and to the same God. The logo's three "streams" also reflect the Trinitarian God who lives and gives life at the heart of all true Christian faith.

Our books are marketed and distributed intensively and broadly through the American Booksellers Association and the Christian Booksellers networks and bookstores; national chains and independent bookstores; Catholic and mainline bookstores; and library and international markets. We are a division of Baker Publishing Group.

Brazos Book Club and Border Crossings

Brazos books help people grapple with the important issues of the day and make Christian sense of pervasive issues in the church, academy, and contemporary world. Our authors engage such topics as spirituality, the arts, the economy, popular culture, theology, biblical studies, the social sciences, and more. At both the popular and academic levels, we publish books by evangelical, Roman Catholic, Protestant mainline, and Eastern Orthodox authors.

If you'd like to join the Brazos Book Club and receive our books upon publication at book club prices, please sign up online at **www.brazospress.com/brazosbookclub**.

To sign up for our monthly email newsletter, Border Crossings, visit **www.brazospress.com**. This email newsletter provides information on upcoming and recently released books, conferences we are attending, and more.

BrazosPress
The Tradition Alive